298

45p

THE VEGETARIAN COOK BOOK 2

All you need to know about buying, storing and preparing wholefoods, plus a wealth of delicious and healthy vegetarian recipes to cater for all occasions.

THE VEGETARIAN COOK BOOK 2

More Delicious and Healthy Recipes for All Occasions

DAVID ENO

THORSONS PUBLISHING GROUP
Wellingborough, Northamptonshire
Rochester, Vermont

Produced in co-operation with
The Vegetarian Society of the United Kingdom Ltd.,
Parkdale, Durham Road, Altrincham, Cheshire

First published March 1986
Second Impression May 1986
Third Impression May 1987

British Library Cataloguing in Publication Data

Eno, David
The vegetarian cook book.
2
1. Vegetarian cookery
I. Title
641.5'636 TX837

ISBN 0-7225-0797-6

Printed and bound in Great Britain

Contents

Introduction

Wholefoods, or natural foods, have become increasingly popular in recent years, and deservedly so because, quite apart from any nutritional or health advantages, they look and taste so much better than the highly refined convenience foods which are heavily advertised, and which food manufacturers would so much rather we bought.

Before the widespread use of modern refining techniques, food additives, and chemicals in agriculture, almost all foods could have been described as wholefoods. A glance at any supermarket shelf reveals that few present-day foods are free of all additives or have not been factory-processed in one way or another. The main objections to this are that processing almost always removes some of the vital nutrients in food, that some food constituents become highly concentrated, perhaps more so than the body can tolerate, and that a selection from some 2000 permitted food additives are incorporated into the food. These include preservatives, stabilizers, anti-oxidants, emulsifiers, artificial dyes, flavouring, and sweetening agents.

Over-consumption of refined foods is thought by many to be one of the factors contributing to the alarming increase in various diseases, such as cancer, arterial sclerosis, heart disease, thrombosis, diabetes, ulcers, dental decay, etc., which afflict 'civilized' societies. There is still conflicting evidence concerning this, but recent advances have exposed some of the dangers of over-refined foods and the food additives, pesticides and antibiotics used in food production.

Whilst millions of pounds are being poured into medical research, it is surprising to find how few medical practitioners attach any importance to diet, apart from its obvious connection with obesity. In contrast, there seems to be a growing awareness of diet and health amongst the general public and a growing reaction against heavily processed convenience foods. Whereas a few years ago it was difficult to buy wholemeal bread, wholemeal flour, brown rice etc., they can now be found in most supermarkets.

The recipes in this book use wholemeal flour in place of white, unprocessed honey and un-refined raw cane sugar in place of refined granulated sugar and syrup. Foods containing additives, or those which are processed or chemically preserved, are replaced by wholegrain foods such as brown rice, wholemeal flour, bread, and pasta, buckwheat, fresh vegetables and fruit, dried beans and pulses, nuts, naturally dried fruit, dairy products and free-range eggs.

The increasing interest in wholefoods is reflected by the growing quantity of books and magazines devoted to the subject, and the increasing number of shops, supermarkets and market stalls selling wholefoods; you should experience no difficulty at all in locating the ingredients mentioned.

Wholefoods look more appetizing, taste better and are more nutritious than refined foods. They provide nourishment in a form and concentration to which the body is accustomed and as you will find, when you try out some of the recipes, their preparation is neither difficult nor time-consuming. The results are interesting enough to tempt even the appetite of the most conservative eater and those trying out a wholefood diet for the first time quickly experience the feeling of increased mental and physical fitness and alertness which confirmed wholefood-eaters take for granted.

Note: All quantities given in the recipes are for 4 people, unless otherwise stated.

1.

INGREDIENTS

All foods should preferably be grown organically to avoid contamination by agricultural chemicals. It is a great advantage to grow your own fruit and vegetables, as this gives you complete control over what could amount to a large proportion of your diet. You can also be sure your produce is fresh and picked in its prime. If you are unable to grow your own it is getting easier to find shops selling organic produce and there has been much publicity recently for organic farming methods, so I'm sure things will improve in this direction still further.

Whole grains and wholegrain foods not only contain more protein, essential oils, vitamins and minerals but also have a higher proportion of roughage or fibre. This is the indigestible component of food which passes straight through us, but which is, nevertheless, a vital constituent of our diet, helping to prevent constipation and other internal disorders.

Brown Rice

Brown rice differs from white rice in that it has not been 'polished' to remove the outer skin. It is this skin which contains much of the goodness of the rice grain. In polishing, the protein, fat, vitamin, mineral and trace element content of rice becomes seriously depleted.

Brown rice is inexpensive and forms the ideal basis for a nutritious diet. For those with sensitive or difficult digestion it is a better staple than potatoes or bread, helping to stabilize and prevent digestive upsets.

The best brown rice to buy is the short-grain type. This has less tendency to become a soggy mass and the grains remain separate. It also seems to have a better flavour. Rice is much cheaper when bought in bulk and will keep for up to six months without losing too much of its nutritive value.

Beans and Pulses

Pulses are a most useful addition to the diet, providing a variety of cheap nutritious dishes. Unlike most other high protein foods they can be stored for long periods without deterioration. Another advantage is that they are comparatively cheap and can even be grown in one's own garden.

While it is true that many pulses do not contain the exact balance of amino acids (the components of protein) required in human nutrition, the missing or inadequate amino acids are readily supplied by other foods such as cheese, eggs and grains, and these can be combined into the same dish or eaten during the same meal. In this way a perfectly adequate balance of amino acids may be assimilated. However, soya beans and mung beans with 61 and 57 per cent protein, which is immediately usable by the body, closely approach meat, which has an average value of 67 per cent, so can be used as direct substitutes.

Although specific pulses are suggested in most of the recipes do not be afraid to experiment and substitute others in their place. Don't forget also that cooking times may need to be adjusted.

Note: Many of the recipes in this book use *pre-cooked* beans. Please check each recipe carefully to make sure you have pre-cooked beans where necessary.

Soaking

All pulses should first be washed in a colander or strainer. They are frequently dusty and lentils in particular often have small stones mixed with them. Pick out any that are bad or discoloured.

Most pulses require soaking for at least 12 hours and preferably for 24. You may find it easier to put several batches of pulses in to soak at the same time, storing those you don't need in the fridge — where they will keep for about five days. Lentils, split peas, aduki beans and black-eyed beans can be cooked without prior soaking. During soaking most pulses double in volume, but soya beans increase by three times.

Cooking

Pulses should be cooked in the same water as that in which

they were soaked so as to retain minerals, vitamins and flavour. Salt should never be added until cooking is finished, as this slows the absorption of water. Thorough cooking until completely soft is essential for palatability and ease of digestion. This means cooking for at least 20 minutes for lentils, half an hour for small beans and one to two hours for larger beans. It is a good idea to cook pulses well in advance of a meal to ensure that enough time is allowed. It is difficult to give precise cooking times, although these are indicated in the recipes, as they tend to vary with age and storage conditions. Where possible it is often a good idea to cook pulses separately from other vegetables.

A pressure cooker is particularly useful with pulses which take a long time to cook, such as soya beans and chick peas, and can reduce the time required by about two-thirds. Excellent stews can also be quickly made in a pressure cooker. Another way to speed up cooking is to grind pulses to flour in a coffee or grain mill. This is useful for soups and stews and does away with the need for soaking, enabling cooking to be completed in 15 to 20 minutes. Ready-ground soya beans, in the form of soya flour, can be bought in most health and wholefood stores. This valuable additive can be used for enriching bread, cakes, muesli and savoury dishes.

When a bean purée is required this can be made either in a liquidizer, a hand soup blender, or by passing through a sieve. A large gravy strainer is also ideal, together with a wooden spoon which is used for rubbing the pulp through. This process is much easier if the pulses are still hot from cooking.

Seasoning
Whereas freshly picked peas and beans are full of their own flavour, and need little treatment apart from light steaming or boiling, dried pulses tend to be bland and require a bold hand with the seasoning to counteract this. Herbs, onions, garlic, and tomatoes blend particularly well with pulses and can be used to intensify flavour, together with freshly ground black pepper and sea salt.

Nuts
Nuts, like all other seeds, contain a store of food accumulated by the plant to nourish its offspring once it has germinated. Proteins, carbohydrates, fats, vitamins, minerals and trace elements are all present, and because the seed of the plant is designed to be compact, these foods are in concentrated form, which also makes them particularly good food for man.

The following is a brief summary of the nuts more commonly grown or imported into this country.

Almonds — There are two types, bitter and sweet. The former are used principally for the production of almond oil, the processing of which removes the highly poisonous hydrogen cyanide which is present in the nut. Almond oil is used for flavouring, and in cosmetics where its softening effect on the skin is particularly valuable. Sweet almonds lack any toxic ingredient and are widely used in cooking. They are rich in fat, protein, the vitamins B_1, B_2, nicotinic acid, and are very rich in the minerals calcium, phosphorus, magnesium and copper. Sweet almonds are cultivated principally in Spain, the South of France, Italy and California. The best almonds are said to come from Malaga.

Coconut — Of tropical origin the flesh contains a rich store of oil, making it highly nutritious. Widely used in its desiccated form in Western cookery, it is rich in iron. It is very good eaten fresh in salads and in desserts.

Brazil Nuts — Are also rich in oil, containing up to 66 per cent, and with 14 per cent protein they also rate as being highly nutritious. Delicious in roasts, rissoles etc.

Filberts, Hazel and Cob Nuts — The hazel is the hedgerow nut of Britain and was widely gathered in the past. The filbert and cob are improved strains, which produce a heavy crop of large nuts. They are rich in vitamin B_1, phosphorus, magnesium and copper. In this country commercial production is mainly restricted to Kent, although because of the heavy demand for them huge quantities are imported from Spain, Italy, France, Turkey and North America.

Peanuts — Harvested from a small annual plant, peanuts are produced below the ground. Rich in oil, and because they are related to the pea family, they are rich in protein (up to 30 per cent). They are also an excellent source of vitamin B_1, B_2, nicotinic acid, B_5, B_6, folic acid, biotin, calcium, phosphorus, magnesium, iron and manganese. Peanut butter is made by removing the skin and grinding the roasted nut. (See page 66.)

Sweet Chestnut — This was introduced into Britain probably by the Romans. Although it grows well in this country large quantities are imported from Spain, hence its other name of Spanish Chestnut. In the southern part of Europe they have been grown for centuries and the nuts ground into flour for use in soups, fritters, porridge, stuffings and stews, whilst the whole nuts are also boiled, roasted, or preserved in syrup (marrons glacés) and eaten whole.

Walnuts — Many fine old walnut trees have been felled for their valuable timber, and because they take fifteen years even to begin fruiting they are not frequently planted. Consequently most of our supplies are imported. The nut is rich in oil, which is used for cooking in France. It contains vitamin C when fresh, also B_1, B_2, B_5, and is rich in phosphorus, magnesium and copper.

The nuts listed above vary considerably in availability and price. In the following recipes they are fairly interchangeable, except for coconut, and so it is possible to use what is most easily available.

Wholemeal Flour
Wholemeal flour, which is recommended for all the recipes in this book, is milled from whole wheat and contains not only the starchy white endosperm found in white flour, but also the germ and husk. The germ gives wholemeal flour more protein and fat, including essential fatty acids, more iron, thiamine, and riboflavin. The husk, once thought to be unimportant because it is indigestible, is a valuable source of fibre. Wholemeal flour makes delicious bread, pastry and cakes and

can be used as a thickening for stews, the base of sauces, etc.

Eggs

Eggs are a concentrated food and a particularly good source of protein. Over 90 per cent of protein present in eggs can be utilized, compared with 68 per cent in meat and 45 per cent in peanuts. Apart from protein, eggs contain useful amounts of vitamins A & D, iron and riboflavin, but no protein.

Although eggs have been listed among foods containing saturated animal fat, which can contribute to hardening of the arteries, they contain only 12 per cent fat, as compared to meat which may contain up to 50 per cent and butter which contains 82 per cent.

Eggs in Cookery — Not only are eggs nutritionally valuable, but they possess many other useful qualities. They help to bind dry mixtures, they form an impervious coating for frying, and they increase the tenacity of dough so that it retains air, increasing lightness. The yolk can be used to emulsify oil, which is useful in mayonnaise and sauces, and they add colour and flavour to all dishes. The longer eggs are cooked the more indigestible they become, but this is less so when they are cooked in a mixture. The white of hard-boiled egg is the most difficult to digest.

Supermarket Eggs — All eggs bought in shops and supermarkets, unless expressly marked otherwise, are obtained from battery hens. Battery hens are kept two or three to a small cage in vast factory-like buildings, leading a thoroughly miserable existence. It is mainly for this reason that I strongly recommend the avoidance of battery eggs.

Free-Range Eggs — Free-range hens are allowed to roam where they can obtain sun, air, and natural foods to supplement their diet. Free-range eggs, though more expensive, are infinitely preferable to battery eggs. They are strong shelled, with richly coloured and flavoured yolks. By buying free-range eggs you can be assured of avoiding antibiotics and chemicals which may be present in battery eggs, and because they are usually produced locally they are fresher than battery eggs, which can be 10 to 14 days old.

Farm Eggs — This term rarely denotes free-range eggs. They are more likely to be battery eggs sold directly from farm to shop. Many shop keepers are confused about the difference between fresh eggs, farm eggs and free-range eggs, so choose your source carefully.

There is no difference between the contents of brown and white eggs. Some breeds of hen lay white eggs, some brown.

Testing for Freshness — Place the suspect egg in a tumbler containing cold water with 1 teaspoon of salt added. One of the following should happen:-

(1) If it rests on the bottom it is fresh.
(2) If it stands on end it is a week or so old.
(3) If it floats with part of the shell above the water it is stale.

Fats, Oils and Dairy Products

Fats and oils are basically different forms of the same substance. They are found in animal products, meat, eggs, and milk, and in some vegetable products such as nuts and seeds. Root and leaf vegetables are very low in fat, as are most fruits. Many sorts of fats and oils are found in food and their precise structure is thought to have a bearing on the amount of cholesterol, another fatty substance, which naturally occurs in our bodies. Saturated fats, as found in red meats and dairy products, are thought to encourage the excessive formation and deposition in the arteries of cholesterol, leading to disease. As widely advertised, unsaturated fats in cooking oils and margarines are thought not to cause this and may even prevent it.

There is still much controversy over fat in the diet but the most important generalizations to emerge from this seem to be that (a) polyunsaturated fats are preferable to saturated fats and (b) a little fat in the diet is preferable to a lot, regardless of whether it is saturated or not.

However, a small amount of fat in the diet is very necessary for the correct absorption of fat-soluble vitamins, so a completely fat-free diet is not desirable. From a gastronomic point of view fats improve the flavour of food by absorbing the essential oils of herbs, seasonings and vegetables, and are vital to certain cooking processes.

Where fat or oil is necessary therefore, use in moderation and use good quality polyunsaturated oils if possible. These include sunflower oil, soya oil, walnut and olive oil (this last one is monounsaturated but may still be used, especially in conjunction with polyunsaturated oils). These will impart the best flavour to food, especially if the very high quality cold-pressed type is used.

For some purposes I think cream and butter are almost indispensable, in soups for instance, and for serving with cooked vegetables, but in these cases I always use them in moderation. Cooking methods which use minimal amounts of fat are also to be preferred.

Dairy products, such as cream and cheese, contain fairly large amounts of fat, but yogurt, cottage cheese, Quark-type soft cheese and skimmed milk are all low in fat. Some low-fat Cheddar-type cheeses are now on the market and there is a whole range of soya-based dairy products, which are low in fat and which are becoming increasingly popular.

Seasonings

Seasonings should complement the natural taste of a dish, not hide it. Be careful not to overseason.

Sea Salt — Contains many trace elements, each important in its own way for the correct functioning of the body. Heavily processed foods often lack these vital elements.

Celery Salt — Is a useful ingredient for seasoning and adding extra flavour at the same time. Make your own by grinding or liquidizing sea salt with celery seed.

Garlic Salt — For a subtle hint of garlic in your cooking. Again you can make your own by grinding sliced garlic and sea salt together in a pestle. Dry the mixture in a warm place and grind again to remove lumps.

Ingredients

Pepper — Always use freshly ground black peppercorns. Their hot spicy flavour is worlds apart from the usual lifeless grey powder. For dishes where you don't want black bits use white peppercorns, although these have less flavour.

Greens

Choose fresh and firm from the shop, or better still grow your own — no others taste quite as good and no amount of careful preparation can cover up for a limp leaf! Cooking should be for as brief a time as possible and in the minimum amount of water. This prevents destruction and the leaching out of vital trace elements and vitamins.

Greens can be quite simply eaten on their own, and correct cooking can transform them into something special. For a quick meal try a small plate of lightly cooked cabbage or your favourite greens served with butter, lemon juice and a little garlic. Melt the butter and squeeze the lemon juice and garlic into it. Grated cheese may be sprinkled on top and a few slices of tomato make a stunning combination with the greens.

Although a recipe may specify one type of greens this is only a suggestion. Most greens can be happily interchanged. Try some of the following:

Cabbages — Also known as brassicas these are many and varied, consisting usually of a much swollen terminal bud or series of buds as in Brussels sprouts. The leaves can be smooth as in the common cabbage or wrinkled like the Savoy.

Spring Cabbage — Is a term applied to young plants whose leaves are less tightly packed, though they are now available for a large part of the year. Most cabbages are best cooked for 5-7 minutes in a minimal amount of water.

White or Dutch Cabbage — Is densely packed and excellent for salads.

Red Cabbage — Is similar to the above, but is a dark purple. Frequently pickled, but also spectacular in salads, or cooked normally.

Kale — Also of the brassica family, has spread out leaves rather than compacted into a bud. The ordinary large leaved kale tends to be tough when cooked, unless small leaves and shoots are chosen. Curly kale is often grown for kitchen use, being more succulent. Some varieties grown as winter greens are useful in winter when other greens aren't available. Use finely shredded young shoots in salads, with plenty of dressing, or shred coarsely and boil in a very little water for 5-10 minutes.

Cauliflower — A flowering cabbage of which the compact flower buds are eaten. The leaves are also excellent eaten as cabbage but removal of the tough midrib of the leaf is advisable.

Broccoli — Similar to cauliflower, though technically winter maturing as opposed to summer and autumn maturing.

Sprouting Broccoli — Has smaller, looser, and more elongated heads of flowers than cauliflower and these are a rich green colour.

Purple Sprouting Broccoli — Is a form of the above with a rich purple bloom on the buds. Cooked lightly and eaten with a little butter it is a delicacy.

Chinese Cabbage — Varieties of *Brassica chinensis* and *pekinensis* are sometimes available on street stalls and in Chinese supermarkets. They may be treated in the same way as cabbage, but one variety frequently seen looks like a cross between lettuce and cabbage and is sold as 'Chinese Leaves'. This is excellent raw in salads or sliced and fried, and can often be found now in high street supermarkets.

Kohlrabi — Or turnip-rooted cabbage is seldom grown nor sold in this country, but is becoming increasingly available. Both leaves and root can be eaten. Treat the leaves as for cabbage.

Spinach — A member of the beet family which has rich glossy leaves and contains more protein and vitamins than most other greens. It is often tinned or frozen as purée, though it is better taken fresh. Spinach is delicious buttered, with a squeeze of lemon juice and garlic.

Sea Spinach — A wild spinach commonly found on cliffs facing the sea. It is variable in habit, and can form dense low-growing plants or lush upright growths, more like cultivated spinach, depending on the habitat. The stems are often tinged with purple and it is from this plant that beetroot is derived. Cook as for spinach.

Turnip — In the same way as beetroot, the tops may be eaten and are occasionally sold as turnip greens. The greens of the turnip's larger counterpart, the swede, may also be treated as spinach.

Seakale Beet — Also known as Swiss Chard, this is a strong growing plant with dark green leaves and massive stalks and midribs which are white and succulent and for which the plant is largely eaten. Cook either whole or chopped until tender (10-15 minutes).

Orache — Occasionally cultivated, though more often found growing as a weed, it is a relation of the spinach family. There are many varieties, fat hen being a common annual weed. Both leaves and flower buds are quite delicious treated as spinach but require only the briefest of cooking (3-5 minutes).

Watercress — A much-neglected source of iron and vitamins, its dark glossy leaves may be cooked in soups, pies and pancakes, or eaten raw in salads.

Mustard and Cress — A relative of watercress, this is excellent for garnishing or mixing into rice dishes. Useful because it is available all year round.

Lettuce — There are again many varieties and although similar to cabbage, in having an enlarged terminal bud, they are not related. Familiar as salad plants, but they may also be cooked. Beware 'bolted' lettuces which can cause illness.

Dandelion — Is little known as a food plant in this country, although it is an excellent source of vitamins and minerals and was widely used by the American Indians. The young leaves chopped and dressed make a very respectable salad. Some of the bitterness can be removed by blanching under large flower pots. The leaves may also be cooked in soups or on their own as spinach.

Stinging Nettle — One of the most abundant and valuable wild greens. Cooking completely removes the sting. Choose only young tips as older leaves have a disagreeable hairy texture.

Many other wild plants may be eaten. For a fuller description of all edible wild plants see Richard Mabey's excellent book *Food for Free* (Collins).

Warning — Although the green parts of plants such as beetroot and turnip may be eaten, do not experiment with plants you are not sure about. The green parts of potato and tomato plants contain poisonous alkaloids which may be fatal. Rhubarb leaves contain oxalic acid which can also be fatal.

Fresh Peas and Beans

Although peas and beans are most often cooked, they can be delicious eaten raw in salads. However, the older they are the less palatable they become and so cooking may be necessary. To get the best possible flavour and texture light cooking only should be given.

Steaming is by far the best method of cooking and young peas and broad beans should be given five to ten minutes, while French beans, mangetout and runner beans should be given up to fifteen minutes. A sprig of mint can be added during cooking.

The simplest way to serve is to toss in butter and sprinkle with sea salt, and this is probably best if you are planning to have a complicated main dish. However if you wish to serve them in a more elaborate way there are some suggestions in the recipes.

Sprouting Beans, Grains and Other Seeds

The beansprouts which are now on sale in many supermarkets and greengrocers shops are grown from mung beans. These are small green beans which are traditional in Chinese cookery. All beans and many seeds can be sprouted with equal success, and several seed companies now sell packets of various seeds specifically for this purpose. The resulting sprouts are sweet and crunchy and highly nutritious. Sprouted beans and grains contain a large proportion of vitamins and are a delicious addition to salads and fried rice dishes. Suitable candidates include: red beans, soya beans, black-eyed beans, chick peas, wheat and grains.

Although special plastic sprouters are available, and make sprouting almost foolproof, with a little more perseverance a jam jar (preferably 2lb/900g size) can be used with equal success. The beans are first soaked overnight and next morning the water is poured away. At this stage it is easiest to fix a piece of muslin across the top of the jar with a rubber band. Keep the sprouts in a warm place, light is not necessary. Wash morning and night by filling the jar with cold water through the muslin and then inverting for a few minutes. When the sprouts have grown to three times the length of the original seed they are ready. This normally takes three to five days.

The sprouts can be used in a number of ways — raw in salads and sandwiches, or lightly cooked in rice dishes, soups, curries etc.

Herbs

Appetizers — Basil, bay, chervil, chives, dill, fennel, garlic, lemon balm, lovage, marjoram, mint, nasturtium flower, parsley, salad burnet, summer savory, tarragon, thyme, lemon verbena.

Bread — Basil, caraway, chives, fennel, garlic, marjoram, parsley, rosemary, tarragon, thyme.

Cakes — Caraway, marigold, rosemary, lemon verbena.

Cheese — Caraway, basil, chervil, chives, dill, garlic, lovage, marigold, marjoram, mint, nasturtium leaves, parsley, rosemary, sage, sorrel, summer savory, tarragon, thyme.

Drinks — Borage, chamomile, bergamot, lemon balm, lemon verbena, mint, rosemary, salad burnet, sweet cicely, tarragon.

Egg Dishes — Basil, bay, chervil, chives, dill, garlic, lovage, marigold, marjoram, mint, nasturtium leaves, sorrel and flowers, parsley, rosemary, sage, salad burnet, summer savory, tarragon, thyme.

Mushrooms — Basil, bay, chervil, chives, dill, garlic, marjoram, parsley, rosemary, sage, tarragon, thyme.

Pasta Dishes — Basil, bay, chervil, chives, fennel, garlic, lemon balm, lovage, marjoram, parsley, rosemary, sage, summer savory, tarragon, thyme.

Potatoes — Basil, bay, chervil, chives, dill, lemon balm, marjoram, mint, parsley, summer savory.

Puddings — Caraway, lemon balm, marjoram, mint, rosemary, sweet cicely, lemon verbena.

Rice Dishes — Basil, bay, chervil, chives, garlic, lovage, marigold, marjoram, mint, nasturtium leaves, parsley, rosemary, sage, sorrel, summer savory, sweet cicely, tarragon, thyme.

Salads — Basil, chervil, chives, dill, fennel, lemon balm, lovage, marjoram, mint, nasturtium leaves, parsley, salad burnet, sorrel, summer savory, tarragon, thyme, lemon verbena.

Salad Dressings — Basil, bay, chervil, chives, dill, fennel, garlic, lemon balm, lovage, mint, nasturtium seeds, parsley, sweet cicely, tarragon, thyme, lemon verbena.

Sandwiches — Basil, chives, dill, fennel, lovage, nasturtium leaves, parsley, salad burnet, sorrel, summer savory, tarragon, thyme.

Sauces — Basil, bay, chervil, chives, dill, fennel, garlic, horseradish, lemon balm, lovage, marjoram, mint, nasturtium seeds, parsley, rosemary, sage, sorrel, summer savory, sweet cicely, tarragon, thyme.

Soups and Stews — Basil, bay, chervil, chives, fennel, garlic, lemon balm, lovage, marjoram, mint, parsley, rosemary, sage, sorrel, summer savory, tarragon, thyme.

Teas — Chamomile, bergamot, fennel seed, lemon balm, lovage, mint, salad burnet, parsley, rosemary, sage, lemon verbena.

Ingredients

Tomatoes — Basil, bay, chervil, chives, fennel, garlic, marjoram, mint, parsley, sage, summer savory, tarragon, thyme.

Vegetables — Basil, bay, chives, dill, fennel, garlic, lemon balm, lovage, mint, parsley, rosemary, salad burnet, sorrel, summer savory, tarragon, thyme.

Vinegars — Bay, chervil, dill, fennel, garlic, lovage, mint, tarragon, thyme.

2.

STORING, PREPARING AND COOKING

Storing Foods

Freshness is of great importance in food, particularly where no artificial preservatives are used. Seeds, grains, pulses, nuts, and root vegetables are designed by nature to last a considerable time, but only when their protective skin is intact. The slightest damage to this can allow air, fungi, and bacteria to enter. The oil in nuts and grains, for instance, begins to oxidize when exposed to air, causing rancidity. This explains why milled or chopped grains, nuts and pulses cannot be kept for more than a few months and should always be kept in an airtight container.

Washed root vegetables bought in supermarkets last only a short time because they are cleaned by abrasive action which often removes most of their skin. Earth is a good sign on root vegetables, so long as it does not conceal rotten patches! Wherever possible root vegetables such as carrots, radishes, and beetroot should be bought with the leaves still attached.

Cool storage conditions are essential for most foods, because this slows chemical breakdown and the action of micro-organisms. Dry conditions also tend to inhibit the growth of bacteria and fungi. For perishable foods a refrigerator set between 3-8°C (37-46°F) is ideal, while for other foods the cool dry airy conditions of the old-fashioned larder are ideal.

With leaf vegetables death begins at the moment of harvesting and enzyme action rapidly starts to destroy the vitamin content. This is another important advantage of growing one's own vegetables, where cooking can follow picking immediately. Any bought vegetable is bound to be at least one day old, and is usually considerably more than this. Wilting and yellowing leaf vegetables have almost certainly lost a great deal of their food value and it is always false economy to buy cut-price fruit and vegetables if they show even the slightest sign of deterioration.

Preparation of Fruit and Vegetables

Having taken some trouble to ensure that raw foods are fresh and wholesome it is important not to waste this effort by incorrect preparation and cooking.

All fruits and vegetables, whether eaten raw or cooked, should first be washed quickly under a stream of cold water. The only exceptions to this are mushrooms, which become waterlogged and should therefore only be wiped carefully with a clean dry cloth. To remove soil use a vegetable scrubbing brush. Special brushes can be obtained from some kitchen-ware shops, although any small scrubbing brush may be used.

Never give prolonged soaking to vegetables as this dissolves out minerals and vitamins. Discard as little as possible, especially with leaf vegetables where the dark outer leaves are rich in minerals and vitamins. Peeling of root vegetables should be avoided as a large portion of the vitamin content is found just beneath the skin. Also removal of the skin makes it easier for the remaining vitamins and minerals to be dissolved out.

Vegetables should only be chopped or shredded immediately prior to cooking or eating. This prevents oxidation of vitamins. Lemon juice used as a dressing can help to stop oxidation and also has a strong anti-bacterial effect.

Cooking

The very worst treatment to give vegetables is to boil them in a large volume of water for a long period. Any prolonged heating destroys the vitamins and the cooking water dissolves away any minerals or vitamins that may be left. If vegetables are to be cooked this is best done in the bare minimum of water, a quarter of an inch (½cm) in the bottom of the pan is usually sufficient if a tight-fitting lid is used.

For this method — which may be used with cabbage, kale, spinach, seakale, carrots, turnips, parsnips, fresh peas and beans of all types, marrow, courgettes or pumpkin — the vegetable should be cut into suitably small pieces with a sharp knife. Cooking should be brief, from 5 to 15 minutes as required, most of the cooking being done by the steam. Because only a little water is used less heat is needed, so keep the heat down low. The water should evaporate almost completely during cooking, making straining unnecessary, thus conserving food value.

As an alternative, steaming is an even better way of cooking and this retains the flavour, texture, appearance and food value of vegetables more than any other method.

One important point to remember with either method is that the water should already be boiling when the vegetables are introduced. This ensures that the enzymes which break down the vitamins are destroyed instantly by the intense heat, rather than being given favourable warm conditions to continue their action while the pan heats up. Soda of any type should never be used when cooking green vegetables and is quite unnecessary as greens cooked quickly will take on a brilliant coloration.

Baking is another useful method of cooking, particularly for potatoes but also for parsnips, turnips, and swedes. Here again, because no water is used and the skin is retained, there is little loss of food value.

Another sound method of vegetable cooking, known sometimes as 'conservative cooking' is literally to stew vegetables in their own juice. The English name derives from the way the flavour and food value is conserved. This method of cooking requires a heavy pan, or a heat-diffusing mat, and a close-fitting lid. Pre-heat a little oil or butter and using a very low heat gently fry the chopped vegetables, stirring occasionally with a wooden spoon. When each piece has a coating of butter place the lid on the pan and continue to cook on a low heat for 10 to 20 minutes. The juices ooze out and turn to steam, which helps with the cooking.

Once cooked, all vegetables, and indeed any food, should be consumed as quickly as possible to avoid any further loss of food value.

Freezing

Although in general all preserved foods should be avoided, freezing — if done properly — does not involve the use of additives or substantial alteration of food value, and so is a valuable method of food storage.

Ready-made but un-cooked rissoles and sausages, and the basic mixtures for these, can be very successfully deep-frozen, which can be a useful time saver. A large batch of the mixture can be made at one time and stored in this way until needed. About double the quantity of herbs as given in the recipe can be used, as freezing tends to reduce their strength. Sausages and rissoles should be laid out individually on a tray and once frozen can be packed into sealed bags or airtight plastic containers.

When using dried beans it can also save much time if they are cooked in large batches and frozen. As these need long soaking and cooking try to cook at least twice the amount stated in the recipe and freeze whatever you don't need. You will soon build up a useful stock for quick soups, stews, salads and pies. Open-freeze by spreading out on a tray and when hard store in airtight bags or food containers. They will keep like this for several months.

3.

UTENSILS

In the kitchen, as in most areas, it really pays to get the best equipment you can afford. While the initial outlay may seem extravagantly large, good quality equipment pays for itself over and over again — not only in durability but from time and sheer frustration saved. Also, with professional quality tools at your fingertips you will feel like a professional and the results you achieve will reflect this.

Saucepans

For all saucepans, and food utensils in general, stainless steel is near perfect. It is a hard metal which is inert to food acids and alkalis, so retains a polished surface which is easy to keep clean and does not contaminate food. Usually all that is required after a soak in hot water and detergent is a wipe with a soft cloth.

When buying pans it is as well to make sure that knobs and handles are hard wearing, or are easily replaceable, for in my experience these are always less durable than the rest of the pan. As well as this you should look for a thick pan with a heavy copper or aluminium conducting base, which will distribute the heat evenly and rapidly.

Ovenware

Quite apart from the ordinary type of pan designed for cooking on top of the stove there is an enormous range of pans and casseroles designed for slow cooking in the oven. These are generally made out of poorer heat-conducting materials, such as cast iron, Pyrex, enamelled iron, pottery etc., and they allow heat to pass less easily in order to cook slowly and evenly. The only things to avoid in this range are enamelled steel, as opposed to the heavier and more durable enamelled cast iron, and coloured enamel on the inside of the pan, which has been shown in some cases to be toxic.

Slow Cooking

One useful device for slowing down cooking on top of the stove is a heat-diffusing mat. This may consist of wire mesh, perforated metal plates or asbestos, although perhaps the last is best avoided for health reasons. The mat slows down the passage of heat into the pan and prevents sticking and burning, particularly with stews, curries, sauces, and in general any dish which uses thickening.

Frying Pans

A pan which is one of my favourites is a cast iron skillet. This is a large heavy pan which can be used on top of the stove or in the oven. It has a closely fitting lid (test just how well this fits before buying) and is something between a frying pan and a saucepan and can be used as such. It is particularly useful for sautéed dishes, casseroles, stews and for anything which requires long slow cooking.

Like the skillet, heavy cast iron frying pans are a delight to use. They cook evenly and hardly ever stick or burn. Most cast iron ware is relatively cheap and durable, although it may crack if dropped on a hard surface.

An entirely different type of frying utensil is the Chinese wok. This is a hemispherical pan of plate steel and comes with a lid and collar for adapting it to use on an ordinary gas stove. It is particularly useful for cooking by a method known as stir-frying, which is used for many Chinese dishes.

When using a wok the ingredients must be finely chopped, the pan heated with some oil or butter, and the cooking brief and accompanied by frequent stirring with a wooden spatula. Although the heat should be fierce the brief exposure ensures that little nutritive value is lost and that food texture is sealed in — as is characteristic of many Chinese dishes. A wok is useful for outdoor cooking on charcoal or on an open fire, where, because of its sturdy nature it is unaffected by extremes of heat or rough treatment.

Steamers

Although special steaming pans can be obtained, a more adaptable alternative is to use one of the inexpensive devices which fit into or on top of pans. One ingenious type fans open to fit any size of pan, while those designed to fit on top of the pan often have a stepped base so that they will fit a range of different sized pans, or may even be stacked on top of each other. Whatever type of steamer is used a closely fitting lid is essential.

Knives

At least one, and preferably more, professional cook's knives are essential. These are the most basic and most useful pieces of kitchen equipment, yet it is surprising how few kitchens can boast even one good sharp knife. Many people mistakenly believe that a sharp knife is dangerous, but a blunt knife can be much more so since it cannot be controlled properly, requiring more pressure, thus increasing the danger of slipping.

The traditional cook's knife is made of carbon steel which sharpens easily to a razor edge, but is quickly corroded and discoloured by damp and acid foods. Stainless steel does not corrode, but requires more frequent sharpening. A selection of both types is probably the best solution. The best method of sharpening is the frequent use of a steel.

Gadgets

Two cheap and highly effective utensils which I use frequently are a garlic press and a lemon squeezer. The garlic press saves the fiddly job of chopping and pulping the garlic. The lemon squeezer, which incidentally comes in orange and grapefruit sizes too, has a number of advantages over the traditional type of squeezer. The top neatly holds half a lemon, the middle section squeezes out and strains every drop of juice, while the bottom cup catches it.

Utensils for Liquidizing

Before electric liquidizers were invented, sieves of various types were used and even today have some advantages. They are cheap, make no noise, and most importantly can be used to separate the skins or seeds of soft fruits. They are also effective for making a very thick purée, which many liquidizers are unable to do. Beans for instance can be puréed without any additional liquid by rubbing through a sieve with a wooden spoon.

Foods which have been puréed with an electric liquidizer can, of course, be strained through a sieve afterwards and one might want to do this with a soup to remove tomato skin or celery fibres. A gadget which neatly achieves the two jobs at once is the hand soup maker which comes with various plates for coarse and fine puréeing and sieving.

Care and Cleaning of Utensils

Wood — The main enemies of bowls, chopping boards and other wooden utensils are excessive dampness and dryness. Never soak them or dry them over a stove or radiator, otherwise warping and cracking will result. Wooden bowls and servers can be rubbed with a little olive oil to protect and polish them after washing.

Steel Plate and Cast Ironware — New baking sheets and tins, frying pans, skillets and woks should first be washed in hot soapy water to remove any lacquer or grease. Dry immediately and rub with vegetable oil then gently heat until a hard coating is achieved. This should be repeated once or twice and not only protects the metal from corrosion, but produces a non-stick finish. When cleaning soak for a few minutes first then use only gentle abrasion from a soft plastic scourer. Harsh scouring is never necessary nor desirable as it spoils the surface.

Stainless Steel — If pans are not allowed to burn and are cleaned inside and out after every use they should never need scouring. Soaking in hot water and detergent for a few minutes should allow any stuck-on food to be removed with a soft cloth. Once scouring is used on a pan the surface is scratched and this increases sticking in future.

Hardened grease, which dulls the outside surface and eventually goes brown, can be effectively removed with a caustic oven cleaner, although it should be remembered that such cleaners can cause dangerous caustic burns to eyes and skin and should be kept well out of the way of children and pets. This treatment should be kept away from plastic knobs and handles and is unsuitable for other metals, which may be attacked, but is very effective on glass and enamel oven dishes which frequently become discoloured. If it really becomes necessary a fine grade of wire wool can be used on stainless steel, followed by a polishing compound which can be obtained from ironmongers.

Knives — As already recommended, a steel such as butcher's use is best for sharpening, and is even effective for the popular serrated bread and carving knives. Never, never use the cheap sharpeners with circular hardened steel plates which grate slivers of metal off your precious knives.

Carbon steel knives must be dried immediately after use or they will discolour. Some discolouring is almost inevitable, but can be cleaned off with abrasive powder, or fine grade wet and dry sandpaper. A little vegetable oil rubbed on will protect from damp while storing. All knives should be stored in a rack, as sharp knives stored in a drawer with other utensils soon loose their edge and may suffer, or cause, damage.

It should be a rule in the kitchen that utensils in general, and knives in particular, should only be used for their intended purpose. This avoids danger and expensive damage to equipment.

4.

BREAKFASTS

Fortified Porridge

This substantial breakfast will keep out the cold on a frosty winter's morning.

1½ pints (850ml) milk or water
4 oz (115g) rolled oats
1 tablespoon raisins
1 apple, peeled and chopped
1 tablespoon hazelnuts, chopped
Sea salt
1 cup cooked brown rice
Honey to sweeten

1. Pour the liquid into a pan and stir in the oats, raisins, chopped apple and nuts, and don't forget a pinch of salt.
2. Bring to the boil then reduce the heat and cook for 3-4 minutes. Next add the rice and cook for a further 2 minutes.
3. Sweeten to taste with honey and serve with milk or cream.

Nut and Raisin Yogurt

(Serves 2)

Simple and delicious — prepare the night before and refrigerate. This recipe is an ideal use for home-made yogurt. See page 71.

½ pint (285ml) natural yogurt
1 tablespoon honey (or to taste)
3 tablespoons raisins
2 oz (55g) chopped roasted hazelnuts

1. Pour the yogurt into a bowl and sweeten to taste with honey. (Honey can be omitted as the raisins provide some sweetness.)
2. Stir in the raisins and chopped nuts and leave overnight.

Note: By morning the raisins will have swelled with some of the liquid from the yogurt, at the same time making the yogurt thick and creamy.

Fortified Yogurt Breakfast

(Serves 2)

1 large eating apple
¼ pint (140ml) natural yogurt
Juice of ½ lemon
2 tablespoons honey
8 tablespoons rolled oats
2 tablespoons chopped hazelnuts

1. Remove the core of the apple and chop half into small pieces. Slice the remaining half and sprinkle with a little of the lemon juice.
2. Mix the yogurt, lemon juice and honey thoroughly until blended together.
3. Stir in the rolled oats and chopped nuts and serve, using the apple slices to decorate the top.

Granola

This crunchy breakfast recipe makes a good snack for any time of day. Several ready-made versions are now on sale in the shops.

4 cups rolled oats
1½ cups desiccated coconut
1 cup sultanas
1 cup wheatgerm
1 cup chopped hazelnuts
1 cup sunflower seeds
½ cup sesame seeds
½ cup bran
½ teaspoon sea salt, finely ground
4 fl oz (120ml) vegetable oil
4 fl oz (120ml) honey

1 Mix the dry ingredients thoroughly in a large bowl.
2 Warm the vegetable oil and add the honey stirring until well mixed.
3 Pour the honey/oil mixture over the dry ingredients and work with the hands until a crumbly mixture is formed.
4 Spread on a lightly oiled baking sheet (or two) and place in the oven at 325°F/170°C (Gas Mark 3).
5 Cook for 15 minutes, turning the mixture with a spatula every few minutes. Towards the end of cooking check more frequently and remove from the oven when light brown. A little care is needed here to avoid burning.
6 When cool store in an airtight jar. Serve with milk or yogurt and for a special breakfast add sliced fresh fruit.

Muesli

(Serves 1)

This recipe needs preparation the night before. The ingredients can be varied and added to, or some omitted, according to taste. The fresh fruit can be apples, pears, peaches, apricots etc.

1 tablespoon hazelnuts or almonds
1 tablespoon vegetable oil
4 tablespoons rolled oats
½ cup finely chopped fresh fruit
1 tablespoon lemon juice
1 tablespoon wheatgerm
1 tablespoon raisins or sultanas
Pinch sea salt
2 teaspoons sunflower seeds
Honey or Barbados sugar (optional)
1 small banana
1 tablespoon cream (optional)

1 Place the nuts in a tray and brush sparingly with vegetable oil. Roast in a moderate oven at 350°F/180°C (Gas Mark 4) for 5 minutes and allow to cool.
2 Place the rolled oats in a bowl and add enough milk to cover.
3 Cover the fresh fruit in lemon juice and add, together with the rest of the ingredients, except for the sweetening and banana, and leave overnight in a cool place.
4 Sweeten to taste and serve topped with some sliced banana and a little fresh cream.

Alpine Breakfast

This quick variation on a well-known theme does not need overnight soaking, as in the previous recipe, yet still provides a nutritious cocktail of minerals and vitamins with which to start the day.

1 cup porridge oats
¾ pint (425ml) milk
2 eating apples
1 banana
2 tablespoons mixed chopped nuts
1 tablespoon fresh lemon juice
1 oz (30g) raisins or sultanas
Raw cane or Barbados sugar to taste

1 Take a small mixing bowl, add the oats and stir in the milk.
2 Quarter the apples, cut out the core and chop, retaining the skin. Slice up the banana.
3 Stir into the oats the apple, banana, nuts, lemon juice, dried fruit, and sugar if desired. Serve straight away.

Coddled Egg

1 Bring a pan of water to the boil then turn off the heat.
2 Put in the egg and leave for 10 minutes. The white will be soft and creamy and more digestible than an ordinary boiled egg.

Scrambled Eggs

(Serves 1)

Knob butter
2 eggs
1½ tablespoons milk
Sea salt and freshly ground black pepper

1 Melt the butter in a pan over a gentle heat.
2 Beat the eggs lightly with the milk in a bowl and season to taste.
3 Pour into the pan and continue to heat gently, stirring all the time with a wooden spatula. Before it has quite set remove from the heat and serve immediately.

Variations:
1 Add a little grated cheese, or yeast extract, or both.
2 Add fried mushrooms with a little chopped parsley.
3 Try cream cheese stirred slowly into the cooked eggs with a touch of garlic.
4 Serve with hot buttered spinach and lightly grilled tomatoes.

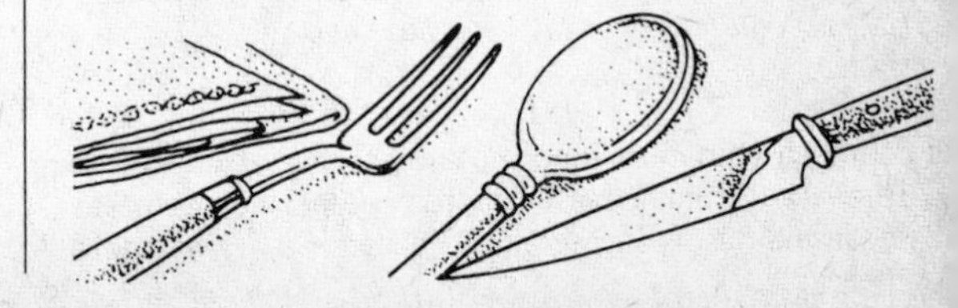

Rice Pancakes

(Makes 6)

4 oz (115g) 81% extraction flour
2 eggs
¼ pint (140ml) milk
Sea salt and freshly ground black pepper
3 tablespoons cooked brown rice
4 oz (115g) mushrooms, chopped
1 small onion, chopped
1 oz (30g) butter or vegetable oil
3 tomatoes
Sprig parsley or watercress

1 Sieve the flour into a bowl and make a well in the centre. Into this break the eggs and beat them, bringing in more flour from the edges until a thick mixture is formed.
2 Add the milk a little at a time until all the dry flour is mixed in.
3 Pour in the rest of the milk and season with sea salt and freshly ground black pepper. Beat until the batter is smooth then add the rice mixing well.
4 Fry the mushrooms and onion together in a little butter or oil, and slice the tomatoes.
5 Heat a frying pan with a little oil and for each pancake add enough batter to cover the bottom. Fry and turn until golden on both sides.
6 Fill the pancakes with the fried mushroom and onion mixture and add a little more seasoning. Top with sliced tomatoes and grill briefly until the tomato is cooked. Garnish with a sprig of parsley or watercress and serve straight away.

Potato Pancakes

For a hearty breakfast try these tasty pancakes.

3 medium potatoes
1 small onion
1 tablespoon wholemeal flour
1 tablespoon wholemeal breadcrumbs
1 tablespoon cream cheese
1 egg
1 teaspoon sea salt
Freshly ground black pepper to taste

1 Grate the potatoes and thinly slice the onion. Mix together.
2 Mix in the flour, breadcrumbs, cream cheese, the lightly beaten egg and seasoning.
3 Stir thoroughly and spoon small dollops into the frying pan, cooking and turning until brown on both sides. Alternatively place all the mixture in the pan at once and make one large pancake.
4 Serve with grilled tomatoes and eggs.

5.

SOUPS AND STARTERS

Soup-making
Home-made soups are superior in flavour, nutritional value and appearance to the commonly available packet and tinned soups. Above all they are inexpensive and most take little time to prepare. There are a few basic points to consider in soup-making and once these are appreciated no difficulty should be found in producing first-class soups.

Soup-making Utensils
The main utensil required is a good sharp knife for chopping vegetables and herbs and a chopping board. The only other essential is a wooden spoon or two for stirring, without scraping your precious pans. There are special soup pans available but any pan which has a good thick bottom will suffice.

One piece of equipment which, although not essential, has revolutionized soup preparation is the liquidizer. This enables smooth soups to be prepared quickly with the minimum of trouble. An alternative to the sieve which does a good job, but takes longer, is the hand soup maker which both pulps and sieves at the same time.

Basic Soup Ingredients
In almost every recipe for soup some form of stock is called for. While meat stocks are frequently used in non-vegetarian recipes, I have always found those made with yeast extract to be extremely successful and convenient. One teaspoon of extract dissolved in 1 pint (570ml) hot water, or the water from boiled or steamed vegetables, is about the right proportion, but remember to reduce the amount of salt used as yeast extract is already quite salty.

Some form of fat or oil is essential in soup-making for dissolving and blending the flavours and gives an overall richness which otherwise cannot be obtained. By far the best fats for soup-making are butter, cream and milk, because of their superior flavour. Avoid cheap blended vegetable oils which can add a very unpleasant flavour. Those wishing to avoid or reduce consumption of animal fats should use high quality vegetable oils such as olive, walnut and sunflower oils.

The Flavouring of Soup
The blending of flavours in a soup is the most important, yet the most difficult part of its making. The careful choice of a few well-flavoured ingredients invariably gives the best results, whilst the more complex the mixture the more confusing and unappetizing to the palate the flavour becomes. The philosophy of throwing everything into the pot may occasionally give edible results but this is always more to do with good luck than good judgement. The simplest of soups, made with very fresh vegetables and herbs, butter or cream, and prepared with the minimum of fuss can be by far the most successful.

Freshness is important with vegetables and it is futile to think of a soup as a way of using up vegetables which otherwise should be heading for the bin. Herbs, too, are much better used fresh and although in the winter you may have to use dried, remember that if they are more than about six months old they are probably past their useful life. Vegetables such as carrots, onions, and celery are frequent ingredients in soups and justifiably so because of their strong aromatic flavours. Garlic is also often used and adds greatly to certain soups, although it should not be used indiscriminately.

Many flavours do not come into their own until they are fully absorbed and blended in fat or oil, which is because the flavours themselves are due to minute quantities of aromatic oily substances.

Serving Suggestions
A Thermos flask filled with soup is ideal for providing a hot and satisfying lunch at a fraction of the cost of eating out. Any smooth soup is suitable for the standard narrow-necked flask, while a wide-necked type is available which will accommodate the lumpy varieties. With a good wholemeal roll or two, perhaps filled with cheese, you have a nutritious and satisfying lunch.

Soups and Starters

Croûtons can be used to make a soup more substantial and are quick to prepare while the soup is cooking. Bread (preferably wholemeal) is cut into thick slices and fried in pre-heated vegetable oil, or better still a mixture of half oil half butter. When the bread is crisp and golden-brown cut into half inch cubes and serve while still hot. Croûtons can be kept for a few minutes in a warm oven.

Cheese can also be used to enrich a soup and improve its nutritional value. A well-matured Cheddar cheese is ideal and can be grated over the soup just before serving.

Always take care to serve soup very hot, preferably into heated bowls. This is particularly important where cheese or croûtons are to be added as the fat content becomes very obvious and off-putting if the soup is lukewarm.

Brown rice can also be used to make soup more substantial and nutritious. Use pre-cooked rice according to taste, or allow 1 oz (30g) per pint of soup, added a few minutes before the soup has finished cooking. Diced potatoes sautéed in butter are also a delicious addition to any soup and make it a meal in itself.

The appearance of food is an important part of its enjoyment. Soup can often be greatly improved by adding a few fresh chopped herbs just before serving. Parsley and chives are the usual choices and are particularly good because of their intense colour and fresh flavour. However, mint, chervil, fennel, lovage, marjoram, and basil can also be successfully used with soups.

Quantities

One last point connected with serving concerns the quantity. If soup is being served with a full meal it is important to serve only a small quantity. Your culinary efforts will not be appreciated by family or guests who are already bloated with large plates of soup, so make this course of exquisite quality but of small quantity. Unless otherwise stated the recipes are suitable for four persons, that is approximately ½ pint (285ml) of soup per person, which is an average serving. Slightly less than this can be allowed if the soup precedes a full meal, while more should be allowed for the hungrier members of the family if the soup forms the main part of a meal.

Quick Stock

2 teaspoons yeast extract
½ teaspoon celery salt
1 pint (570ml) hot water

1 Dissolve the yeast extract and celery salt in the hot water. Use in any recipe where stock is needed. As this is quite salty do not add further salt to a recipe without tasting first.

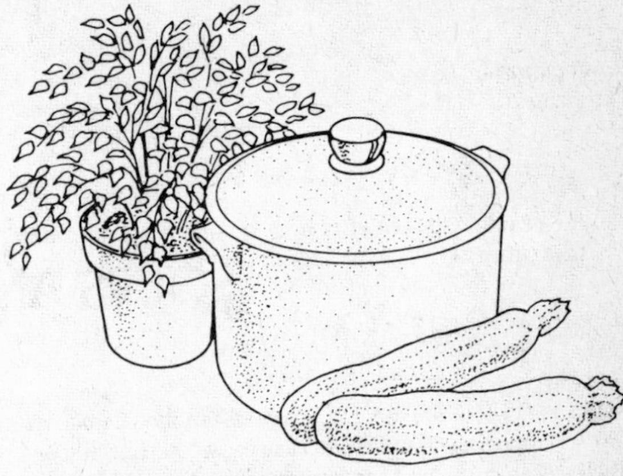

Vegetable Stock

This useful stock can be made with any left over or damaged vegetables which need only coarse chopping.

2½ pints (1.4 litres) water
1 onion
2 celery stalks with leaves
1 large carrot
1 tablespoon yeast extract

1 Heat the water in a pan and add the coarsely chopped vegetables, including the celery leaves. Simmer for 45 minutes.
2 Strain off the liquid and throw away the vegetables. Add the yeast extract. Use wherever stock is required.

Croûtons

2 slices wholemeal bread
2 oz (55g) butter

1 Fry thick slices of wholemeal bread in butter and when crisp and brown cut into ½ inch (1.5cm) cubes.
2 Sprinkle over soup just before serving.

Cheese Croûtons

2 slices wholemeal bread
2 oz (55g) Cheddar or Gruyère cheese

1 Toast the bread on both sides then cover one side with grated or thin slices of cheese and grill until brown.
2 Cut into 1 inch (2.5cm) squares and float on soup before serving.

Summer Soup

An appetizing soup using garden-fresh vegetables for a light summer lunch.

1 medium onion
1 oz (30g) butter
1 bunch young carrots, finely chopped
4 oz (115g) new potatoes, finely diced
1 small turnip, finely chopped
2 pints (1.1 litres) vegetable stock
3 oz (85g) shelled peas
3 oz (85g) runner beans, sliced
Freshly ground black pepper and sea salt
1 sprig mint
1 crisp lettuce heart
1 tablespoon 81% extraction flour
1 sprig parsley

1 Sauté the onion in the butter over a gentle heat and add to this the carrots, potatoes and turnip. Continue to cook until the vegetables just begin to brown.
2 Add the stock, peas, runner beans, and seasoning, and simmer for fifteen minutes.
3 Now add the chopped mint and lettuce heart and cook for a further five minutes. During this time remove a few tablespoons of the liquid and mix with the flour in a cup. Stir this back into the soup and make sure that it is brought back to the boil for at least two minutes.
4 Taste and add further seasoning as required, sprinkle with chopped parsley and serve.

Spring Onion and Herb Soup

1 bunch spring onions
1 oz (30g) butter or vegetable oil
1 carrot
1 stick celery
2 pints (1.1 litres) vegetable stock
1 sprig each marjoram, thyme, fennel
Parsley and watercress, chopped

1 Remove the bulbs from the onion tops and chop very finely. Sauté in the butter and add the chopped carrot and celery. Continue to cook until the vegetables soften but do not allow to brown.
2 Add the stock, the chopped herbs and the coarsely chopped watercress. Season and allow to simmer for 10 minutes.
3 Add the chopped onion tops and allow a further 5 minutes cooking. Test seasoning and serve.

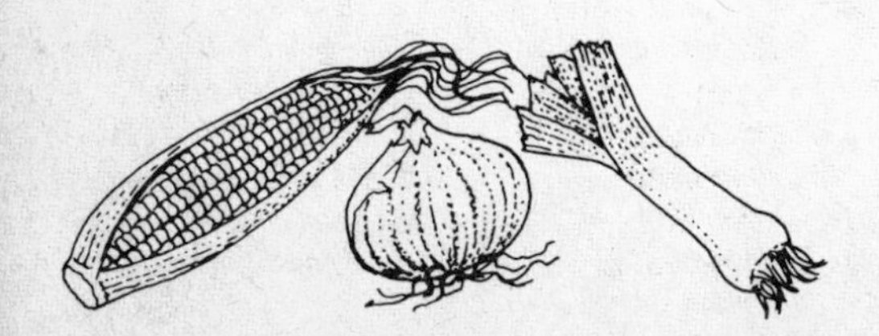

Garlic Soup

This is an extremely pungent soup which may be eaten purely for enjoyment, or used medicinally to relieve heavy colds and nasal congestion.

4 to 8 cloves garlic
½ oz (15g) butter or olive oil
1½ tablespoons 81% extraction flour
1 pint (570ml) milk
1 pint (570ml) vegetable stock
2 teaspoons parsley, chopped
Sprig sage
Sea salt and freshly ground black pepper

1 Pulp the garlic with a press and fry gently in the butter or oil. After a few minutes add the flour and slowly stir in the milk.
2 Add the rest of the ingredients and simmer for 15 minutes.
3 Check the seasoning and serve very hot, either alone or with cheese.

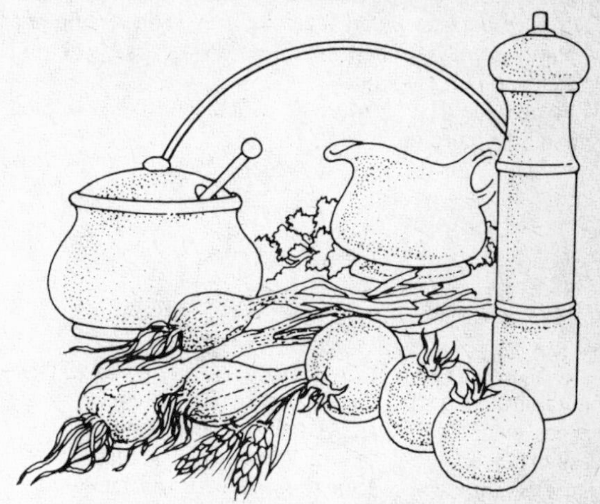

Mushroom and Lemon Soup

This can be eaten hot or cold.

2 oz (55g) butter
1½ oz (45g) wholemeal flour
1 pint (570ml) vegetable stock
½ lb (225g) mushrooms
½ pint (285ml) milk
Sea salt and freshly ground black pepper
Juice of 1 lemon
¼ pint (140ml) double cream

1 Melt the butter in a pan, stir in the flour and cook gently for a few minutes. Add the stock and bring to the boil, stirring frequently.
2 Mince or finely chop the mushrooms and add these to the stock.
3 Add the milk and season with salt and pepper and lemon juice to taste. Simmer for 5 minutes and stir in the cream.
4 Chill at this stage if serving cold; otherwise re-heat gently, without boiling, and serve.

Soups and Starters

Rice and Vegetable Soup

This is a really good way of using up cooked left-over rice and vegetables. Rice fried with vegetables or any selection of rice and vegetables cooked separately can be used.

1 medium onion
1-2 cloves garlic
1 tablespoon vegetable oil
2 cups of mixed cooked rice and vegetables
2 pints (1.1 litres) vegetable stock
Sea salt and freshly ground black pepper
Sprig parsley
Chilli powder

1 Fry the chopped onion and a clove of pulped or sliced garlic in a little vegetable oil using a large pan.
2 Next add the rice and vegetables, which have been thoroughly liquidized with the vegetable stock.
3 Season with freshly ground black pepper and sea salt and add the chopped parsley and the smallest pinch of chilli powder, but exercise great caution here. The very tip of a pointed knife is the best measure to use, as it is easy to ruin your soup with too much.
4 Re-heat the soup and taste to see if any further seasoning is required before serving.

Onion Soup

This soup is simplicity itself to prepare and yet is one of the most delicious.

2 oz (55g) butter
¾ lb (340g) onions, chopped
1 tablespoon 81% extraction flour
2 pints (1.1 litres) vegetable stock
1 teaspoon thyme, chopped
Sea salt and freshly ground black pepper

1 Melt the butter in a heavy pan and fry the onions. Cook until the onion just begins to brown.
2 Stir in the flour which will absorb the fat and prevent it floating to the top of the finished soup.
3 Add the stock and the chopped thyme and season to taste. Continue to simmer gently for 20 minutes and serve very hot with croûtons or cheese.

Celery Soup

2 oz (55g) butter
1 medium onion
1 large head celery
2 carrots
½ pint (285ml) milk
1½ pints (850ml) vegetable stock
2 teaspoons fresh herbs, chopped
Sea salt and freshly ground black pepper
Sprig of parsley, chopped

1 Melt the butter in a saucepan over a gentle heat and fry the finely sliced onion until soft but not brown.
2 Chop the celery, wash well, and retain the young leaves, as these add extra flavour. Chop into small pieces and add to the onion. Continue to fry for about 5 minutes over a gentle heat.
3 Scrub the carrots and slice finely.
4 Add the milk, stock, the herbs and the carrot and bring to the boil. Simmer for 15 minutes then sieve or liquidize.
5 Bring back to the boil and season to taste. Just before serving add the chopped parsley.

Beaten Egg Soup

2 pints (1.1 litres) vegetable stock
1 tablespoon tomato purée
1 tablespoon yeast extract
4 eggs
1½ tablespoons wholemeal flour
3 tablespoons herbs, chopped
Sea salt and freshly ground black pepper

1 Heat up the stock and dissolve in it the tomato purée and yeast extract.
2 Beat the eggs, blending in the flour, and when the stock is simmering slowly pour in the egg mixture. Keep stirring the soup and thin strands of egg will coagulate to form a noodle-like substance.
3 Serve sprinkled with the chopped herbs.

Spinach Cream Soup

This recipe can be used with sorrel, seakale, or watercress but the seasonings should be adjusted accordingly.

½ lb (225g) spinach, fresh or frozen
1 oz (30g) butter
1 medium onion
1 clove garlic
1 tablespoon 81% extraction flour
1½ pints (850ml) milk
3 tablespoons double cream
Pinch grated nutmeg
Sea salt and freshly ground black pepper

1 Cook the spinach for 10 minutes or until soft.
2 Melt the butter in a pan and sauté the finely chopped onion and garlic, but do not let them brown. Stir in the flour and cook for a minute or two.
3 Now slowly add the milk, stirring continuously and bring to the boil. Allow to thicken then remove from the heat, stirring in the spinach and cream.
4 Purée, using a sieve or liquidizer, and re-heat without allowing it to boil. Add a pinch of nutmeg and season as necessary. Serve with croûtons.

Carrot Soup

2 onions
1 lb (455g) carrots
2 oz (55g) butter
½ tablespoon wholemeal flour
1 pint (570ml) vegetable stock
½ tablespoon thyme, chopped
1 bayleaf
Sea salt and freshly ground black pepper
1 pint (570ml) milk

1 Chop the onion finely and grate the carrots. Cook in the butter over a gentle heat for 10 to 15 minutes with a lid on the pan.
2 Stir in the flour and add the stock, thyme, bayleaf and seasonings. Cook for a further 10 minutes.
3 Remove the bayleaf and sieve or liquidize. Return to the pan and add the milk. Bring to the boil, adjust the seasoning and serve.

Cream of Cauliflower Soup

1 medium cauliflower
1 bayleaf
1 onion
1 stick celery
1 oz (30g) butter
4 tablespoons wholemeal flour
1 pint (570ml) milk
1 pint (570ml) vegetable stock
Sea salt and freshly ground black pepper
1 teaspoon French mustard
1 teaspoon yeast extract

1 Quarter the cauliflower and cook gently with the bayleaf in 1 inch (2.5cm) of water for 15 minutes.
2 Purée half of the cauliflower, taking care to first remove the bayleaf.
3 Chop and fry the onion and celery in the butter and when soft stir in the flour and cook for a few minutes.
4 Add the milk slowly, stirring constantly to avoid lumps. Next stir in the cauliflower purée, and finally the stock, mixing together thoroughly. Season with salt and pepper, French mustard and yeast extract.
5 Carefully break up the florets of the remainder of the cauliflower and sprinkle into the soup. Avoid boiling after this stage or the florets will break up. Serve with croûtons.

Cream of Mushroom Soup

¾ lb (340g) mushrooms
2 teaspoons fresh lemon juice
Sea salt and freshly ground black pepper
2 oz (55g) butter
1 medium onion
1 clove garlic
1 tablespoon wholemeal flour
1 pint (570ml) milk
1 pint (570ml) vegetable stock
1 teaspoon thyme, chopped

1 Chop the mushrooms into small pieces, place in the soup pan and sprinkle with lemon juice, salt and pepper.
2 Add the butter, chopped onion and garlic and begin to heat very gently with a lid on the pan. After about 15 minutes of cooking much of the juice of the mushrooms should have oozed out.
3 Now stir in the flour and little by little the milk, stirring and heating until a smooth mixture is obtained.
4 Add the stock and thyme and bring to the boil. Allow to cool slightly and sieve or liquidize, adding the cream at the same time.
5 Re-heat and adjust the seasoning before serving, but on no account allow to boil.

Soya Vegetable Soup

A quickly made and nutritious soup.

2 tomatoes
1 onion
3 tablespoons olive oil or butter
4 tablespoons soya flour
2 tablespoons 81% extraction flour
1½ pints (850ml) vegetable stock
1 teaspoon yeast extract
Sea salt and freshly ground black pepper
1 tablespoon fresh chopped herbs

1 Skin the tomatoes by placing in boiling water for half a minute. Chop the onion and tomatoes finely and sauté in the oil in a large pan.
2 When well cooked stir in the soya flour and wheat flour and cook for a few minutes longer.
3 Add the stock little by little, stirring continuously to avoid lumps. When all the stock is added bring to the boil, add the yeast extract and simmer for 15 minutes.
4 Season with salt and pepper and any fresh chopped herbs you wish. If you prefer a completely smooth soup liquidize or pass through a sieve.

Soups and Starters

Lentil Soup

1 large tomato
1 onion
1 clove garlic
2 tablespoons vegetable oil
1½ pints (850ml) vegetable stock
4 oz (115g) red lentils
1 stick celery with leaves
2 tablespoons parsley, chopped
Sea salt and freshly ground black pepper

1 Peel the tomato by placing in boiling water for half a minute. Slice and fry the onion, tomato and garlic in the vegetable oil and when soft add the stock and lentils.
2 Chop the celery finely, including the leaves, and add to the soup with the parsley, salt and pepper. Bring to the boil and simmer very gently for 30 minutes
3 Now place in a liquidizer and blend for 2 minutes or pass through a sieve.
4 Re-heat, adjust seasoning and serve.

Pea Soup

½ lb (225g) dried peas
2 pints (1.1 litres) vegetable stock
1 large onion, chopped
2 leeks, chopped
2 oz (55g) butter
1 carrot
1 potato
3 sticks celery
Sea salt and freshly ground black pepper

1 Soak the peas overnight.
2 Cook the soaked peas in the vegetable stock until soft, which should take between 1 and 2 hours or in a pressure cooker about half an hour.
3 Meanwhile sauté the onion and leeks in the butter and when cooked add about ½ pint (285ml) stock from the peas and the chopped or diced carrot, potato and celery. Cook for 20 minutes.
4 Add the cooked peas and the rest of the stock and simmer for a further half an hour over a very low heat.
5 Liquidize or pass through a sieve and season with freshly ground sea salt and pepper to taste.
Note: This soup is also delicious when made with chick peas.

Tomato Soup

For best results use very ripe well flavoured tomatoes.

1 medium onion
1 oz (30g) butter
1½ lbs (680g) ripe tomatoes
1 large potato
1 pint (570ml) vegetable stock
1 teaspoon parsley, chopped
1 teaspoon basil, chopped
¼ pint (140ml) double cream (optional)
1 teaspoon honey or raw cane sugar
Sea salt and freshly ground black pepper

1 Fry the sliced onion in the butter and add the washed and halved tomatoes. With a lid on the pan continue to cook until the tomatoes become a pulp, stirring occasionally to avoid browning.
2 Peel and chop the potato and add it to the pan with the rest of the ingredients. Simmer until the potato is soft then liquidize and reheat.
3 Add salt and pepper to taste and further sugar or honey if the soup is at all acid. Serve with a dollop of cream if liked.

Potato Soup

A thick and satisfying soup for cold winter days.

1 medium onion
2 sticks celery with leaves
1 oz (30g) butter or oil
1½ pints (850ml) vegetable stock
2 tablespoons parsley, chopped
1 teaspoon marjoram, chopped
1 bayleaf
Sea salt and freshly ground black pepper
1½ lbs (680g) potatoes
½ pint (285ml) milk
1 tablespoon wholemeal flour

1 Chop the onion and celery and sauté in the butter or oil over a gentle heat for 10 minutes, using a pan with a closely fitting lid. Stir occasionally to prevent browning.
2 Add the stock, herbs, bayleaf and seasoning but save a little parsley for later. Add the peeled and sliced potatoes and allow to simmer until the soup is soft, which should take about 20 minutes.
3 Meanwhile stir the milk into the flour to produce a lump free mixture and when the potato is cooked stir this into the pan and bring back to the boil.
4 Allow to cool slightly and liquidize or pass through a sieve, re-heat, add further seasoning as necessary and sprinkle with chopped parsley before serving.

Leek and Potato Soup

A delicious and distinctively flavoured thick soup.

1 lb (455g) leeks
½ clove garlic
1 oz (30g) butter or oil
1 lb (455g) potatoes
1½ pints (850ml) vegetable stock
½ pint (285ml) milk
2 tablespoons 81% extraction flour
½ teaspoon celery salt
Freshly ground black pepper
1 tablespoon parsley, chopped

1 Clean the leeks and chop into small pieces. Sauté together with the sliced garlic in the butter.
2 Peel and slice the potatoes and add with the stock before the leeks begin to brown. Cook for about 20 minutes or until the potatoes are soft.
3 Add the milk to the flour in a bowl and beat until smooth. Stir this into the soup and bring back to the boil.
4 Liquidize or sieve and season to taste. Stir in the freshly chopped parsley before serving.

Mixed Vegetable Soup

A thick chunky and sustaining soup, ideal for winter meals.

2 tablespoons butter
2 large mushrooms
1 large onion
2 carrots
1 stick celery
1 cup cooked red kidney beans
2 pints (1.1 litres) vegetable stock
1 teaspoon thyme, chopped
1 teaspoon marjoram, chopped
Sea salt and freshly ground black pepper
½ lb (225g) potatoes
2 small Jerusalem artichokes
2 tablespoons red lentils
1 tablespoon wholemeal flour

1 Melt the butter and sauté the chopped mushroom, onion, carrots and celery and the cooked beans, until they are soft but not beginning to break up.
2 When the vegetables begin to brown add the stock, herbs, seasoning, diced potato and artichoke and the lentils and cook for 30 minutes.
3 Mix the flour with a little of the stock from the pan to make a lump-free paste. Dilute with more stock until quite liquid and stir into the pan. Bring back to the boil and test the seasoning before serving.

Bortsch (Beetroot Soup)

This recipe can be used with raw beetroot, or pre-cooked, but not pickled.

1 lb (455g) beetroot
1 onion
1 carrot
3 tomatoes
2 sticks celery
2 pints (1.1 litres) vegetable stock
1 clove garlic
Sea salt and freshly ground black pepper
1 teaspoon soft brown sugar
1-3 teaspoons wine vinegar
¼ pint (140ml) soured cream
1 tablespoon chives, chopped

1 Peel the raw beetroot and grate into a pan.
2 Grate the onion and carrot and chop the tomatoes and celery and add to the pan. Add the stock, pulped garlic and seasoning and simmer for 1 hour. Alternatively, if using pre-cooked beetroot, grate and proceed as before, omitting ¼ of the stock and cook for only 30 minutes.
3 Add the sugar and then the wine vinegar and seasoning to taste. Serve with a dollop of soured cream and a few chopped chives for each portion.

Basic Nut Soup

This is particularly good with almonds and hazelnuts.

1 oz (30g) butter
1 onion
1 carrot, chopped
1 large potato, chopped
1 pint (570ml) vegetable stock
2 oz (55g) nuts
1 teaspoon parsley, chopped
½ teaspoon honey
Sea salt and freshly ground black pepper

1 Melt the butter in the pan and fry the chopped onion over a gentle heat until soft. Add the chopped carrot and potato and the stock and simmer for 20 minutes.
2 When this is ready liquidize together with the nuts.
3 When smooth add the parsley, honey, and seasoning, and bring to simmering point before serving.

Chestnut Soup

½ lb (225g) chestnuts or 6 oz (170g) purée
2 medium onions
1 stick celery
1 carrot
1½ oz (45g) butter
2 pints (1.1 litres) vegetable stock
1 teaspoon marjoram
Sea salt and freshly ground black pepper

1 Break the chestnut skins with a fork to prevent explosions and bake in a moderate oven for 15 minutes. When cool enough peel away the shell and inner skin.
2 While the chestnuts are baking chop the vegetables finely and cook in the butter over a gentle heat until they begin to brown.
3 Add the peeled chestnuts or purée, the stock, the marjoram and seasoning and cook for 30 minutes or until the chestnuts begin to break up. Liquidize or sieve, reheat, adjust seasoning and serve.

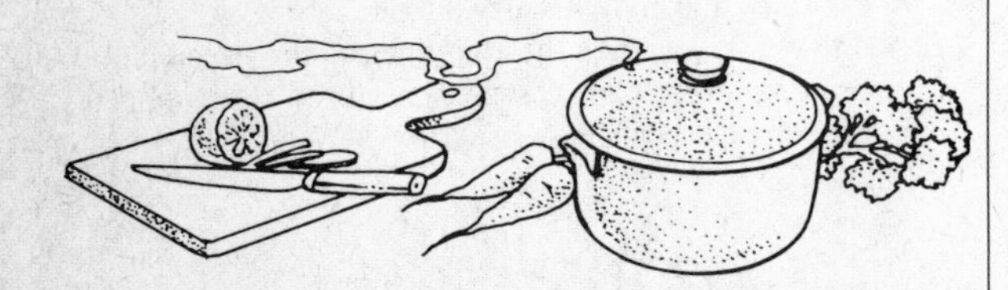

Gazpacho (Spanish Iced Soup)

This soup, made without cooking, is served ice-cold. It makes a most refreshing summer meal and should be accompanied by fresh baked crusty rolls and butter.

1 lb (455g) ripe tomatoes
½ pint (285ml) tomato juice
½ small cucumber, diced
4 tablespoons olive oil
3 spring onions
2 tablespoons white wine vinegar
2 oz (55g) black olives (optional)
2 cloves garlic
Sprig each of parsley and mint
Sea salt and freshly ground black pepper
½ pint (285ml) iced water and ice-cubes

1 Immerse the tomatoes in boiling water for half a minute to loosen their skins, then peel and chop finely or liquidize for a few seconds, but avoid turning into a purée.
2 In a bowl mix with the tomatoes, the tomato juice, the diced cucumber, olive oil, finely chopped spring onions, the wine vinegar and the olives if liked.
3 Pulp or crush the garlic and add together with the chopped herbs and seasoning.
4 Refrigerate for at least half an hour and before serving crush or liquidize the ice-cubes and stir into the soup with the iced water.

Mixed Herb Soup

This can be made with the mixture of herbs suggested or with an equal quantity of a single herb.

2 medium-sized onions
1 stick celery
2 oz (55g) butter
1 clove garlic
2 tablespoons wholemeal flour
2 pints (1.1 litres) vegetable stock
Bunch of mixed lovage, parsley, thyme and tarragon
Sea salt and freshly ground black pepper

1 Chop the onion and celery very finely. Sauté in the butter, adding the crushed garlic, and cooking until soft.
2 Stir in the flour and cook for a minute or so, then add the stock, little by little at first, stirring all the time.
3 Chop the herbs finely and add.
4 Simmer for 15 minutes and season according to taste, then serve.

Note: For a richer soup, stir in 2 tablespoons double cream just before serving.

Mushroom and Leek Soup

2 carrots
2 leeks
1½ pints (850ml) vegetable stock, or water plus 2 teaspoons yeast extract
½ teaspoon chopped parsley
½ lb (225g) mushrooms
Sea salt and freshly ground black pepper

1 Chop the carrots and leeks.
2 Bring the stock to the boil, add the carrots, leeks and parsley and cook until the vegetables are done.
3 Strain off the liquid and add to it the thinly sliced mushrooms. Cover the pan and simmer gently for 30 minutes, adding salt and pepper to taste.

Roasted Nuts

Freshly roasted nuts eaten hot make a really appetizing starter or snack. The best nuts to use are almonds, peanuts, hazel and cashew nuts. There are two methods:

1 For cooking in the oven, usually the most successful way, use a shallow tray or flat tin and spread a single layer of nuts on it. Sprinkle lightly with a little vegetable oil and salt to taste. Cook in an oven set at 350°F/180°C (Gas Mark 4) until

browned. Open the oven every 3 to 4 minutes and turn the nuts by shaking the tin. Total cooking time is usually about 10 minutes, and here a word of caution: nuts are very easy to burn and once blackened taste revolting, so ideally you should hover close to the oven until they are done.
2 For cooking in a frying pan, the oil and salt are added in the same way, and here a gentle heat is essential, combined with almost continual stirring to prevent uneven cooking.

Nut Pâté

½ lb (225g) nuts
2 tablespoons wholemeal flour
2 teaspoons fresh herbs, chopped
Sea salt and freshly ground black pepper
2 eggs, separated
4 oz (115g) mushrooms
1 tablespoon vegetable oil
¼ pint (140ml) milk
1 tablespoon tomato purée

1 Grind the nuts in a liquidizer, adding a few at a time with the flour to keep the mixture dry. Turn into a bowl and mix with the herbs, seasonings and egg whites.
2 Fry the finely chopped mushrooms in the oil and add these to the mixture.
3 Beat the egg yolks with half of the milk and tomato purée. Stir into the mixture, adding if necessary a little more milk to achieve the consistency of mashed potato.
4 Pack the mixture into a well-greased ovenproof dish and cover with foil. Bake for 1½ hours at 300°F/150°C (Gas Mark 2) and allow to cool before turning out. Slice and serve with salads or as a starter.

Hummus

This is a sensational dip or spread which you just can't stop eating! Be sure the chick peas are really mushy before liquidizing, and use good quality olive or vegetable oil.

½ lb (225g) chick peas
Juice of 1 lemon
¼ pint (140ml) vegetable oil
2 cloves garlic, pulped
4 tablespoons tahini
Sea salt
Mint, chopped

1 Soak the chick peas for 24 hours then cook until soft, which will take at least 3 hours or 1 hour in a pressure cooker. When they are really soft strain them but save the cooking water.
2 Save a few chick peas and deep-fry for decoration later. Put the rest in a liquidizer and blend to a smooth paste, adding the lemon juice and some of the cooking water if the mixture begins to clog.
3 Slowly add the oil while liquidizing, then the garlic, tahini and salt to taste.
4 Turn into a serving bowl and decorate with the fried chick peas and a sprinkling of chopped mint.

Red Bean Pâté

1 onion
2 tablespoons vegetable oil
4 oz (115g) mushrooms
2 sticks celery
2 cloves garlic
1 cup red kidney beans, soaked overnight
2 teaspoons tomato purée
1 teaspoon yeast extract
1 tablespoon parsley, chopped
4 oz (115g) stoned black olives
Sea salt and freshly ground black pepper

1 Fry the onion in the oil and add the chopped mushrooms, celery and pulped garlic.
2 Add the soaked beans with the water they were soaked in and boil until cooked, which will take about 1½ hours or less in a pressure cooker.
3 When the beans are really soft and still hot pass them through a sieve and stir in the tomato purée, yeast extract, parsley, chopped olives and seasoning. Place in a greased dish and do not serve until completely cool.

Egg Spread with Olives

Instructions for making the mayonnaise used in this recipe are on page 38.

1 large egg
4 oz (115g) olives
2 oz (55g) butter
2 tablespoons mayonnaise
1 tablespoon parsley, chopped
Sea salt and freshly ground black pepper

1 Hard boil the egg and when quite cold chop finely.
2 Remove the stones from the olives and chop the olives into small pieces.
3 Soften the butter and blend into the other ingredients. Serve on crackers, ryebread, or in sandwiches.

Lentil and Olive Pâté

2 medium onions
2 cloves garlic
2 oz (55g) butter
½ lb (225g) red lentils
2 oz (55g) fresh wholemeal breadcrumbs
2 tablespoons tahini (or peanut butter)
1 tablespoon fresh thyme, chopped
1 tablespoon chervil, chopped
1 tablespoon parsley, chopped
Sea salt
Freshly ground black pepper
3 tablespoons fresh lemon juice
4 oz (115g) black olives

1 Sauté the chopped onions and garlic in the butter until soft.
2 Cook the lentils in plenty of water for 20 minutes, then drain and add the fried onions and garlic.
3 Stir in the fresh breadcrumbs, tahini, herbs, seasonings and lemon juice and purée using a sieve or liquidizer.
4 Stone and chop the olives and stir in. Place the mixture in a serving dish and refrigerate before use. Can be used in the same way as red bean pâté.

Mushroom Cocktail

¾ pint (425ml) natural yogurt
½ tablespoon olive oil
1 tablespoon fresh lemon juice
1 teaspoon honey
1 tablespoon chopped chives
1 tablespoon chopped parsley
Sea salt, to taste
Few crisp lettuce leaves
6 oz (170g) button mushrooms
Paprika

1 Blend the yogurt, oil, lemon juice, honey, herbs and salt to taste.
2 Shred the lettuce finely and half-fill four glasses with it.
3 Thinly slice the mushrooms and stir into the dressing. Spoon into the glasses and top with a little paprika to serve.

Deep Fried Mushrooms

This recipe can be used for an appetizing hors d'oeuvre or as a side dish for a main meal. It can also be served with tartare sauce or garlic mayonnaise (see page 38). Allow 2 oz (55g) mushrooms per portion.

½ lb (225g) small button mushrooms
Wholemeal flour, as necessary
Sea salt and freshly ground black pepper
1 egg, beaten
Wholemeal breadcrumbs, as necessary
Vegetable oil for deep frying
Sprig parsley
1 lemon

1 Wipe the mushrooms clean and dust them with seasoned flour.
2 Dip in the beaten egg and coat with breadcrumbs.
3 Deep fry the mushrooms until they begin to turn golden, drain and serve, garnished with a sprig of parsley and a slice of lemon. Squeeze the juice from the rest of the lemon to sprinkle over the mushrooms.

Herb Cheese

This recipe produces a cheese similar to the Ilchester herb cheeses, sometimes known as potted cheese. Various herbs or combinations of herbs can be tried.

½ lb (225g) good quality Cheddar cheese
Small tin evaporated milk
1 teaspoon Marmite
½ cup herbs, chopped

1 Grate the cheese into a bowl and add the milk and Marmite.
2 Warm very gently over a pan of hand-hot water, stirring until the ingredients blend. Too great a heat will coagulate the cheese.
3 Stir in the herbs and allow to set in individual pots or a large bowl.

Variation: For Garlic Cheese, follow the above recipe using 2-4 cloves of garlic crushed with a little salt.

Cream Cheese Cups

1 small onion
2 tablespoons chopped parsley
6 oz (170g) cream cheese
Lemon juice
Sea salt and freshly ground black pepper
12 mushroom cups
Paprika

1 Chop the onion finely and mix with the parsley and cream cheese.
2 Add lemon juice, salt and pepper to taste and fill the mushroom cups with the mixture.
3 Sprinkle with paprika and serve.

Marinated Mushrooms

This recipe is best served as part of a mixed hors d'oeuvre.

4 tablespoons olive oil
4 tablespoons red wine vinegar
4 peppercorns, crushed
¼ pint (140ml) water
½ teaspoon salt
1 clove garlic
2 teaspoons lemon juice
½ lb (225g) button mushrooms
1 tablespoon chopped parsley

1 Combine all the ingredients except for the mushrooms and parsley, and boil in a pan for 10-15 minutes.
2 Meanwhile chop the parsley and cut the stalks off the mushrooms. Add the mushrooms to the pan and boil for a further 3 minutes, then stir in the parsley and leave to cool.
3 Serve when thoroughly chilled, with a little of the marinade.

Herb Potato Cakes

The herbs for these potato cakes can be selected to taste; parsley, chives, tarragon, chervil and thyme are all safe to start with!

1 lb (455g) potatoes
Butter
Sea salt and freshly ground black pepper
3 tablespoons fresh herbs
Wholemeal flour
1 egg, beaten with 2 tablespoons milk
Wholemeal breadcrumbs

1 Boil the potatoes, then mash with a generous knob of butter. Season with salt, pepper and finely chopped herbs.
2 From the mashed potato into flat cakes and leave to cool.
3 When reasonably firm dust with flour, dip in the beaten egg and milk mixture and cover with breadcrumbs. (Freeze at this stage if desired.) Then fry in a little vegetable oil until golden and serve immediately.

6.

SALADS

The benefits to health of regularly eating fresh uncooked food can be considerable and it is well worth getting into the habit of eating some raw food each day, even if this requires an effort at first. The vitamin content of raw foods is higher than in cooked foods. Consequently one can improve one's intake of these vital nutrients, which keep the chemistry of the body functioning normally, and help protect against infection and illness.

The roughage or fibre content of raw food also tends to be higher, which is not only beneficial to teeth and gums but is vital to the effective working of the digestive system, preventing certain types of ulcer, constipation and other disorders which may have far-reaching effects on the rest of the body.

Raw foods tend to be filling, whilst not containing large amounts of carbohydrate or fat. This makes them ideal not only for slimmers, but also for the rest of us who eat more than we really need.

Finally, by increasing the proportion of raw food in the diet, we can be sure of reducing the amount of food additives and toxins we take in.

Eating More Salads

One of the easiest ways of introducing salads into your normal diet is to serve them either as starters or side dishes with your usual meals. When combining salads with other dishes consider the overall effect. For an already complicated main course a simple bowl of green salad may be all that's needed; where a number of salad dishes are to be used as hors d'oeuvre, for a main course, or for a buffet or picnic, try to make each bowl as individual, yet as simple as possible. Variety really does add much of the spice in cooking and much of the enjoyment of eating a well prepared meal is to find each mouthful a completely different experience.

Salad-making Equipment

The most basic equipment is a chopping board, a peeler or peeling knife, and one or more very sharp cook's knives. Some form of grater is essential: the normal hand type is quite adequate for small quantities but for anyone who is going to feed regularly on salad I would recommend a rotary hand grater or shredder (a number of types are now on the market), or for frequent entertaining the slicing and shredding attachment for a kitchen mixer. A salad shaker is also a cheap and very useful item for drying lettuce and other leafy vegetables.

Salad Ingredients

Where salt and pepper are called for sea salt and freshly ground black or white peppercorns are preferable. Oil and vinegar are frequent requirements in salads and their dressings. Here it is worth obtaining some really good cold-pressed olive or sunflower oil. Ground nut oil, which is the cheapest and most commonly available, has a poor flavour and adds nothing to a salad. White wine vinegar has the finest flavour and is best for salad use, although herb vinegars are also excellent.

The following lists some of the ingredients which can be used.

Green vegetables — Lettuce, watercress, savoy cabbage, white and red cabbage, Chinese cabbage or Chinese leaves, chicory, endives, mustard and cress, land cress, corn salad, dandelion (forced and blanched), Brussels sprouts, and the young leaves of spinach, kale, sprouting broccoli (including the heads), seakale beet, celery, turnips, spring onions, nasturtium and sorrel.

Root vegetables and tubers — Raw carrot, beetroot, swede, turnip, celeriac, and parsnip are delicious grated in salads while in cooked form they can be marinated or otherwise dressed. In addition potatoes and Jerusalem artichokes can be used in a number of ways.

Peas and beans — Peas are particularly good raw in salads, as are young broad beans. Peas, broad beans, French and runner beans can also be cooked and eaten cold with various dressings, and all dried beans can be cooked and eaten in the same way.

Fruits — Almost all fruit can be used in salads, in particular tomato, pepper, apple, orange, peach, avocado and pineapple. Pineapple deserves a special mention because of its sweet sharp flavour which blends particularly well with other salad ingredients. Dried fruits such as raisins, dates and apricots are also good.

Nuts and seeds — Nuts such as hazels, peanuts, almonds and cashews, and seeds such as sunflower, pumpkin and sesame, can be used raw or are especially good when lightly roasted with a little salt and vegetable oil in a shallow tray. The smaller seeds take only a minute or so in a moderate oven whilst the nuts take from five to ten minutes and should be checked frequently to avoid burning, which happens all too easily.

Herbs and flowers — Herbs should be considered an essential part of a salad and the thoughtful use of a few herbs can completely transform even the simplest of meals. Only fresh herbs are really suitable for use in salads. While parsley, thyme, sage and marjoram are available in the summer, it is easy enough to grow these and many others in pots on a well-lit kitchen windowsill through the winter.

For use in salads the following are most useful: parsley, thyme, mint, chives, marjoram, basil, tarragon, chervil and savory.

Flowers such as the following are also good to use in salads — marigold petals, dandelion petals, elderflowers, chrysanthemum petals and rose petals.

Cheeses — The use of all types of cheese in salads helps to balance the meal by providing protein. Don't forget the soft cheeses, cottage and curd cheese, and the various herb cheeses which can be bought or made at home.

Winter Salads

There are many good things available in the winter from which to make salads. Carrots, turnips, swede and other root vegetables, apples, onions, winter lettuce, endives, kale, Brussels sprouts, cabbage, cress, parsley and thyme and more can be used to add variety to the winter diet.

Salad Preparation

As with all types of food, ensuring good quality and freshness of the ingredients is one of the most basic steps in preparation. Simple dishes are often the most successful if the ingredients are carefully chosen and prepared and well presented. Even if you have to pay a little more for fresh top-quality foods, the extra is rarely wasted.

Thorough washing is particularly important with foods which are to be eaten uncooked. All vegetables and fruit should be washed under a fast running stream of cold water. This helps to remove bacterial spores and the eggs of parasites and also residues of sprays (if not organically grown) and pollutants from the air. Prolonged soaking, however, is not a good thing as the vitamins and minerals dissolve in the water. All salad ingredients should be stored in a cool place 4-10°C (39-50°F) but on no account allow to freeze as this destroys the texture and flavour.

To revive lettuce and all leafy vegetables wash under cold water and place in a covered bowl in the refrigerator. After an hour or so the leaves will be crisp and fresh. This also works well with fresh herbs.

Preparation of salads should take place as near to the time of eating as possible to ensure the minimum of deterioration. Only a very sharp knife should be used for leafy vegetables to help prevent bruising, and once cut they should be dressed immediately with an acid dressing (containing citrus juice or vinegar) to prevent oxidation and halt enzyme action which destroys the vitamins.

Dressings — Salad should always be served with some form of dressing. In most cases a simple French oil and vinegar dressing is adequate. Apart from enriching the flavour of the salad, the acidity of the vinegar helps to preserve the vitamin content.

Marinating Vegetables

This is a method of serving lightly-cooked vegetables cold as a salad dish. The best candidates for this treatment are beetroot, young broad beans still in their pods and French beans, although others could be tried. Vegetables should be lightly steamed; as soon as they soften allow to cool. The beetroot should be diced while beans can be cut into pieces.

While the vegetables are cooking prepare a bowl of dressing as follows. Rub the bowl with a cut clove of garlic. Mix one part of best wine vinegar to three parts olive oil, a small amount of sugar or honey, a little salt and a few whole peppercorns and coriander seeds. Add chopped parsley and into this mixture stir the cooked vegetables. Leave overnight or for several hours, stirring occasionally.

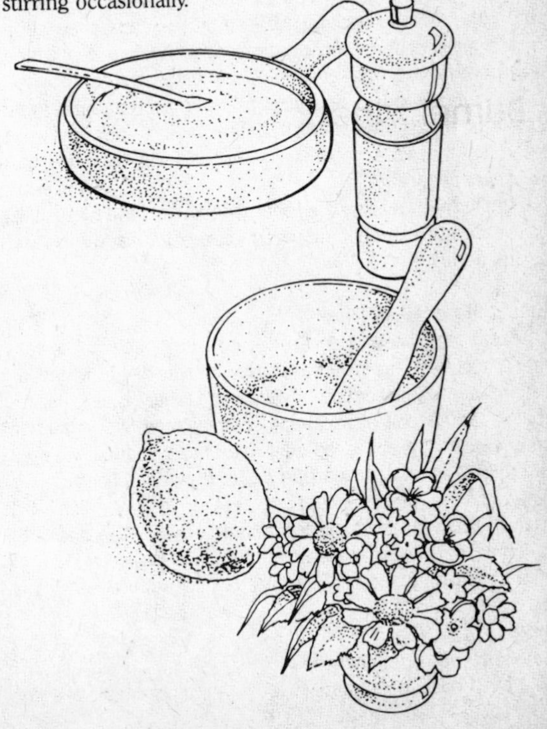

Herbed Oils

Oils, and for the same reason butter, are excellent for dissolving and dispersing the flavour of herbs to maximum advantage. This is because their flavours is almost entirely due to the presence of aromatic oils which combine more readily with oil or fat than with water.

Herbed oils can be used for making salad dressings, soups, sauces, and for general cooking. Use only good quality vegetable oil, preferably cold pressed olive, sunflower or corn oil.

The most useful oils are those flavoured with basil, oregano or marjoram, bay, garlic, thyme and tarragon. A screw-top jar is used for the extraction of the flavour: the jar should be filled with herbs and the oil poured over.Leave in a warm dark place for a week and if the flavour is not strong enough after this time use fresh herbs and leave for a further period. This can be repeated as often as necessary.

Garlic Wine Vinegar

Vinegars can be made with a variety of herb flavours. They are useful in making pickles, salad dressings, sauces, and for flavouring. I often find that a few drops of vinegar are a great improvement to a soup, and herb vinegar is particularly good for this.

5 cloves garlic
1 pint (570ml) red wine vinegar

1 Crush the garlic and add to the vinegar in a saucepan. Heat until almost boiling and then stand until quite cool.
2 Strain and bottle.

Burnet Vinegar

1 pint (570ml) salad burnet leaves
¾ pint (425ml) white wine vinegar
¾ pint (425ml) medium sweet white wine

1 Wash the burnet leaves and place in a sterilized 2 pint (1.1 litre) jar.
2 Mix the vinegar and wine and heat in a pan until almost boiling.
3 Pour over the leaves, seal the jar, and stand for 3 weeks before using.

Tarragon Vinegar

1 pint (570ml) tarragon leaves
¾ pint (425ml) red wine
¾ pint (425ml) red wine vinegar

Follow the same procedure as for Burnet Vinegar (above).

Oil and Vinegar Dressing

This simple dressing can be used on almost any type of salad. The only ingredients are oil and vinegar, which must be good quality cold-pressed olive or sunflower oil, and white wine, cider or herb vinegar. The proportion can be anything from two parts oil to one of vinegar to six parts oil to one of vinegar, which should be shaken together in a bottle before use. Alternatively the oil and vinegar can be served in separate bottles, which allows for individual taste.

Oil and Lemon Juice Dressing

Make sure to use good quality oil, preferably cold-pressed olive, walnut, or sunflower oil.

1 tablespoon fresh lemon juice
6 tablespoons olive oil
Sea salt
A little crushed garlic to taste

1 Shake all the ingredients together in a suitable small bottle or container. The lemon juice can be wholly or partly replaced by white wine vinegar.
2 Keep cool in the fridge and shake well before use. Keeps for several days.

Mayonnaise

Real mayonnaise can be made at home and is well worth the small amount of effort involved. A liquidizer or mixer can speed things up, but patience is the main virtue when mixing mayonnaise. It is also important that all ingredients should be at room temperature.

1 egg yolk
2 tablespoons lemon juice or cider vinegar
1 cup vegetable oil
½ clove of garlic (or to taste)
Sea salt

1 Whisk the egg yolk in a bowl, or beat with a fork, adding a little of the vinegar or lemon juice.
2 Begin adding the oil drop by drop, beating furiously until thickening is detected. Continue to beat, now adding the oil in a slow trickle.
3 When all the oil is added, which takes at least five minutes by hand, add the rest of the ingredients and mix well.

Note: If the oil is added too quickly, or if the bowl is not really clean, the oil will separate into globules, and beat as you may will not thicken to a creamy texture. If this happens all is not lost. Begin again with a clean bowl and fresh egg yolk, adding the separated mixture drop by drop as if it were the oil. Prevention is better than cure so always proceed very slowly and patiently in the initial stages.

To keep the mayonnaise, store in a screw-topped jar in the fridge. As it has no artificial preservatives it will only keep for about 5 days.

Eat with fresh boiled asparagus tips, globe artichokes, raw or boiled cauliflower, with plenty of greens, all manner of salads, vegetable pies, fennel, boiled eggs, watercress, French beans, peas, carrots, boiled rice, corn on the cob, etc.

Ailloli

Ailloli is made with the reckless addition of more garlic to the above recipe. For best effect add as much as you or your guests can take. Start the bidding at two cloves! In Provence a dish called Ailloli Garni is made. This is a sparkling array of fish and raw and cooked vegetables of every kind, including the occasional snail, and a huge bowl of ailloli. With the addition of French crusty bread the feast can begin! (The fish and snails may be omitted!)

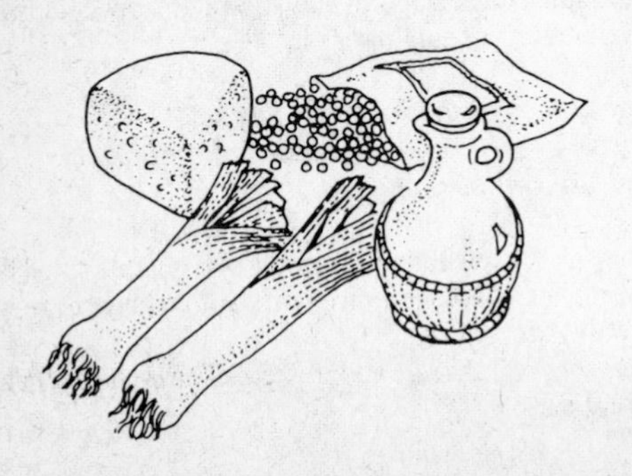

Aillaide

This recipe uses the mayonnaise from the recipe above.

1 oz (30g) hazelnuts, roasted
1 oz (30g) walnuts
1 cup mayonnaise
1 clove garlic

1 Remove any skins left on the nuts by soaking in boiling water for 1 minute then rubbing dry with a cloth.
2 Pound the nuts in a mortar with a little sea salt and when reduced to a fine meal add the mayonnaise and the crushed garlic.

Green Mayonnaise

A small bunch fresh herbs
3 spinach leaves
1 cup mayonnaise

1 Choose a selection of fresh herbs and blanch with the spinach for two minutes in boiling water.
2 Pound to a paste with a mortar and pestle and blend into the basic mayonnaise mixture. Alternatively, you can do the whole job in a liquidizer.

Yogurt and Cucumber Dressing

Yogurt makes a good dressing for most salads and can be used plain or with chopped herbs added — applemint and chives are particularly good. See the recipe for home-made yogurt on page 71.

¼ cucumber
2 tablespoons chives, chopped
1 cup natural yogurt
Sea salt

1 Peel the cucumber and dice finely. Chop the chives.
2 Mix all the ingredients together and season to taste with a little sea salt.

Yogurt and Onion Dressing

4 spring onions
1 cup natural yogurt
½ clove garlic
Sea salt

1 Finely chop the spring onions, bulbs and greens, and stir into the yogurt.
2 Crush the garlic with a little sea salt and add to the yogurt, adding more salt if necessary.
3 Leave to stand for at least half an hour before serving.

Tomato Juice Dressing

½ cup tomato juice
¼ cup wine vinegar
1 cup olive oil
½ teaspoon clear honey
2 tablespoons parsley, chopped
1 teaspoon chives, chopped
Sea salt

1 Beat the tomato juice, wine vinegar and olive oil together and sweeten to taste with a little honey.
2 Add the chopped herbs and season with sea salt.

Oil-less Mayonnaise

This is a quick and easy dressing to make with a liquidizer and is much less fattening than real egg mayonnaise.

2 eggs
2 tablespoons white wine vinegar
4 tablespoons fresh yogurt
½ teaspoon honey
½ clove garlic
Sea salt

1 Hard boil the eggs and when quite cool peel and place in a liquidizer.
2 Add the wine vinegar, fresh yogurt, honey, garlic and a little salt. Liquidize for at least 3 minutes to get rid of any lumps.

Blue Cheese Dressing

4 oz (115g) blue cheese
1 cup natural yogurt
1 tablespoon parsley, chopped
¼ clove garlic
Sea salt

1 Slice the cheese and place in a liquidizer with the yogurt.
2 Add the chopped parsley, crushed garlic and a little salt to taste, and liquidize until quite smooth.

Herb Dressing

½ tablespoon chopped thyme (or lemon thyme)
1 tablespoon chopped chives
1 tablespoon chopped parsley
¼ pint (140ml) natural yogurt
1 teaspoon vegetable oil
Grated rind ½ lemon
1 teaspoon clear honey
1 teaspoon lemon juice
Sea salt and freshly ground black pepper

1 Mix the finely chopped herbs and place in a screw-top jar.
2 Add all remaining ingredients and shake to blend. Season to taste and refrigerate until needed.

Mushroom Dressing

(Serves 8)

Good for crisp green salads.

8 spring onions
½ lb (225g) button mushrooms
2 teaspoons mustard
4 tablespoons lemon juice
1 teaspoon salt
½ teaspoon pepper
8 tablespoons olive oil

1 Chop the onions finely with a sharp knife and thinly slice the mushrooms.
2 Whisk together the other ingredients, then stir in the onion and mushrooms.
3 Refrigerate for 2 hours, stirring once or twice before using.

Honey and Lemon Dressing

This can be used for any salad, but is particularly good with watercress.

4 tablespoons olive oil
4 tablespoons fresh lemon juice
2 tablespoons honey
Freshly pulped garlic, to taste

1 Place all ingredients in a screw-top jar and shake until well mixed and the oil has broken up. Shake again before serving.

Honey and Yogurt Dressing

This again is very adaptable but is good with cooked salad ingredients, such as beans, leeks, cauliflower, aubergines, etc.

2 tablespoons honey
1 tablespoon lemon juice
1 small carton natural yogurt
2-4 tablespoons chopped fresh herbs

1 Dissolve the honey in the lemon juice, then stir into the yogurt.
2 Add the well chopped herbs. These could be parsley, chives, mint, fennel, basil, etc., the quantity according to strength and taste.

Salads

Green Salad

This is the simplest way of serving leafy vegetables and may be used as part of a main course salad, or as a side dish for pizza, pasta or almost any other hot dish. Select from the following:-
Lettuce, watercress, endive, spinach, chicory, cress, dandelion (blanched), sorrel, cabbage, or kale. With plants such as spinach, sorrel and kale, the leaves must be very young to be palatable.

The trick of making the most of this type of salad is to combine two contrasting salad plants, that is, contrasting in colour, texture or flavour, and to remember that some form of simple oil and vinegar dressing is essential. Chopped herbs also help to add a special touch.

Watercress and Orange Salad

1 bunch watercress
Olive oil
Lemon juice
1 sweet orange
1 teaspoon chopped fresh mint

1 Thoroughly wash the watercress and remove the larger stalks.
2 Dress with a few teaspoons of oil and a few drops of lemon juice, and place in a bowl.
3 Thinly slice the orange and remove peel and pips. Decorate the top of the dish by arranging the orange slices in a circle overlapping each other and sprinkle with chopped mint.

Cucumber Salad

The cucumber may be peeled but there is no real need for this. The skin may be scored with a fork which gives a decorative effect when sliced. Slice the cucumber very thinly and arrange in a shallow dish. Sprinkle with salt, oil, and a few drops of vinegar and then with chopped chives.

Tomato Salad

Firm, good flavoured tomatoes are essential for this salad.

1 lb (455g) firm tomatoes
2 tablespoons fresh chopped herbs
Freshly ground black pepper
Olive oil
Sea salt

1 Slice the tomatoes thinly and arrange on a shallow dish.
2 Sprinkle with fresh chopped herbs, basil is best, but parsley, chives or chervil will do.
3 Season with freshly ground black pepper.
4 When ready to serve sprinkle with a few drops of olive oil and some sea salt. Serve immediately as the salt soon makes the tomatoes soft and watery.

Mushroom Salad

½ lb (225g) mushrooms
Juice of 1 lemon
4 tablespoons olive oil
1 clove garlic
1 bunch parsley, chopped
Sea salt and freshly ground black pepper

1 Choose large fresh button mushrooms and slice vertically without removing the stalks.
2 In a small bowl mix the lemon juice with the olive oil and pulped garlic. Pour this mixture over the mushrooms and sprinkle with chopped parsley, salt and pepper.

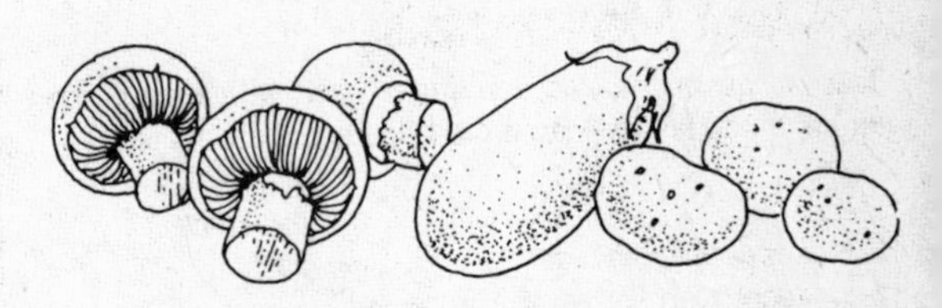

Cabbage and Apple Salad

White, green or red cabbage work equally well in this recipe, or different sorts can be combined.

½ lb (225g) cabbage
2 large eating apples
Juice of 1 lemon
Sea salt and freshly ground black pepper
1 tablespoon salad oil
1 teaspoon cumin seeds
1 tablespoon chives, chopped
2 tablespoons hazelnuts, roasted

1 Shred the cabbage finely with a sharp knife or a rotary shredder.
2 Remove the apple cores but retain the skin. Grate and treat immediately with lemon juice to prevent browning.
3 Mix the apple and cabbage and season with sea salt and pepper and sprinkle with the oil and cumin seeds.
4 Garnish with chopped chives and roasted hazelnuts.

Lettuce and Red Bean Salad

1 crisp lettuce
½ onion
1½ cups red kidney beans, cooked
½ cup oil and lemon juice dressing
Sprig mint

1 Shred the lettuce coarsely and mix with the finely sliced onion.
2 Add cooked beans and toss with an oil and lemon juice dressing.
3 Decorate with a few leaves of mint.
Note: To vary the recipe use any other type of cooked dried beans or cooked fresh broad beans.

Mixed Bean and Onion Salad

1 cup aduki beans
1 cup black-eyed beans
1 cup vegetable oil
1 onion
Olive oil
Sea salt
1 tablespoon fresh herbs, chopped

1 The beans should be cooked until fairly soft, but not crumbling apart. Drain thoroughly and if the two sorts were cooked separately, mix together.
2 Take half of the beans and fry them in ½ inch (1.5cm) of oil, then remove from heat.
3 When completely cool mix with the remainder of the beans and stir in the finely chopped onion.
4 Dress with a little olive oil and serve sprinkled with sea salt and fresh chopped herbs.

Beansprout Salad

2 cups fresh beansprouts
1 small lettuce or cabbage
Bunch spring onions
½ red pepper
½ green pepper
French dressing

1 Mix the beansprouts with the coarsely shredded greens and chopped spring onions.
2 Decorate with thinly sliced red and green pepper and serve with a French dressing.

Easy Marinated Salad

1 lb (455g) tomatoes
½ lb (225g) mushrooms
3 tablespoons white wine vinegar
4 tablespoons olive oil
1 tablespoon thyme, chopped
Sea salt and freshly ground black pepper to taste

1 Using a sharp knife thinly slice the tomatoes and mushrooms.
2 Place these, together with the rest of the ingredients, in a plastic container with an airtight lid and turn gently to distribute the oil and vinegar.
3 Refrigerate salad until needed, turning occasionally.

Diced Mixed Salad

This salad takes some time to prepare, but is well worth the trouble.

2 sweet apples
Juice of 1 lemon
½ lb (225g) firm tomatoes
1 red pepper
1 green pepper
3 sticks crisp celery
1 onion
1 large carrot
1 tablespoon olive oil
Small bunch of herbs for garnish

1 Dice the apple into ¼ inch (7mm) cubes and dress immediately with 1 tablespoon of the lemon juice.
2 Dice the rest of the ingredients to the same size, and mix thoroughly with the rest of the lemon juice and the oil.
3 Decorate with freshly chopped herbs.

Note: Other ingredients can be added or substituted, including — avocado, cucumber, courgettes, radishes, mushrooms, celeriac, cauliflower and pineapple.

Greek Salad

1 large green pepper
2 large firm tomatoes
1 large onion
2 oz (55g) olives
Soft white or Feta cheese
Oil and vinegar dressing

1 In a salad bowl make layers of sliced green pepper, tomatoes, and onion.
2 Add a few olives and top with some soft white cheese. (Cottage or curd cheese are suitable as well as the Greek Feta cheese.)
3 Dress with olive oil and a little vinegar or lemon juice.

Russian Salad

This recipe is a good way of using up left-over cooked vegetables such as peas, beans, carrots, turnips, potatoes, Jerusalem artichokes, asparagus etc.

2 cups cooked mixed vegetables
1 onion
4 tablespoons mayonnaise (see p. 38)
1 tablespoon parsley, chopped

1 Make sure the cooked vegetables are completely cool.
2 Chop the onion and mix with the vegetables and mayonnaise.
3 Sprinkle over the chopped parsley and serve.

Potato Salad

For a really successful potato salad waxy potatoes, which don't break up when cooked, are essential. Recommended varieties are Maris Piper, Jersey Royal, and Pentland Lustre if you can get them.

½ lb (225g) potatoes
Sea salt and freshly ground black pepper
½ onion
1 tablespoon parsley, chopped
½ cup mayonnaise (page 38)

1 Scrub the potatoes and cook in their skins, preferably by steaming. When cool, peel and dice or slice them.
2 Sprinkle with salt and pepper and a few pieces of very thinly sliced onion and some of the chopped parsley.
3 Pour over the mayonnaise and mix gently so that the potato is coated without being broken up.
4 Garnish with the rest of chopped parsley to serve.

Grated Carrot Salad

2 large carrots
Sea salt and freshly ground black pepper
1 orange
½ tablespoon olive oil

1 Grate the carrots finely and season with salt and freshly ground pepper.
2 Cut one half of the orange into slices and extract the juice from the other.
3 Dress the carrots with a few drops of olive oil and the freshly squeezed orange juice.
4 Turn thoroughly to distribute the dressing and arrange on a shallow dish decorated with a few thin slices of orange.

Grated Beetroot Salad

Raw beetroot can be treated in exactly the same way as the carrot in the last recipe, although a slightly coarser grater is best. The best beetroot variety for raw eating is 'Cook's Delight'. The dressing can be the same and a good effect is created by arranging the carrot and beetroot on the same dish.

Apple and Walnut Salad

2 sharp eating apples
Juice of 1 lemon
2 sticks celery
2 oz (55g) walnut halves
Yogurt or mayonnaise dressing

1 Core and peel the apples and cut into rings. Dip each ring immediately into a bowl containing lemon juice.
2 Arrange on a shallow dish with the chopped celery and walnut halves. Serve with a yogurt or mayonnaise dressing.

Coleslaw

This well-known salad, although often bought ready made, is easy to prepare at home and is much better fresh. The chief component is white cabbage and it is essential that this is very finely shredded so that there are no lumpy bits. The coarse grating plate on a rotary grater is ideal, an ordinary grater is rather hard on the knuckles! Use plain or garlic mayonnaise (see page 38). The other ingredients can be varied, but I usually use the following:

1 small white cabbage
1 medium carrot
1 small onion
Sea salt and freshly ground black pepper
½ cup mayonnaise

1 Grate the cabbage and carrot and finely slice and chop the onion with a sharp knife.
2 Season with sea salt and black pepper and mix in the mayonnaise.

Note: As a variation French dressing can be used. Green or even red pickling cabbage can also be used with equal success and give interesting visual effects.

Cauliflower Salad

The slicing plate on a rotary or electric grater is really essential for preparing this salad. The cauliflower must be very fresh and creamy white.

1 small cauliflower
Sea salt and freshly ground black pepper
½ cup lemon juice dressing
1 tablespoon parsley, chopped

1 Using the rotary grater thinly slice the cauliflower florets.
2 Season with salt and pepper and turn in the dressing until completely coated. Garnish with chopped parsley.

Onion and Rice Salad

Cold rice salads are good for buffets, parties, packed lunches and picnics. They can be made with any combination of cooked brown rice and cooked beans, chopped or grated carrot, mushrooms, onion, tomato, cucumber and pepper, etc., fresh herbs and mayonnaise or dressing. This and the following recipe provide two quite different variations.

Bunch spring onions
2 tomatoes
2 courgettes
Bunch radishes
2 cups cold cooked brown rice
2 tablespoons fresh herbs, chopped
1 cup garlic mayonnaise
½ teaspoon sea salt

1 Chop the spring onions and tomatoes and dice the courgettes. Remove the leaves from the radishes but leave them whole, unless they are very large.
2 Mix all the ingredients together in a large bowl, making sure the mayonnaise is well distributed. This will keep in the fridge for a day or two, although if this is anticipated the tomatoes are best left out.

Rice and Bean Salad

1 onion
½ cucumber
1 red pepper
2 oz (55g) black olives
2 cups cooked brown rice
1 cup cooked red kidney beans
½ teaspoon sea salt
Juice of 1 lemon
3 tablespoons olive oil

1 Chop the onion, cucumber and red pepper into small pieces. Cut the olives in half and remove the stones.
2 Mix with the brown rice and beans in a large bowl. Sprinkle on the sea salt, lemon juice and olive oil and stir well.

Spinach Salad

1 lb (455g) raw fresh spinach
1 small onion
2 large tomatoes
⅓ cup olive oil
Juice of 1 lemon
1 clove garlic
Sea salt and freshly ground black pepper
2 hard-boiled eggs

1 Wash the spinach well in cold running water, picking out any weeds, and leave to drain in a salad shaker.
2 Using a sharp knife shred the spinach finely.
3 Chop the onion and tomatoes and mix with the spinach.
4 Make a dressing with the oil, lemon juice, and garlic, adding salt and pepper to taste. Pour the dressing over the spinach and serve decorated with slices of hard-boiled egg.

Cabbage and Bean Salad

1 cup cooked red beans
1 red pepper
3 cups finely shredded cabbage
1 cup mustard and cress
½ cup oil and lemon dressing
1 clove garlic

1 Cook the beans by soaking overnight and boiling in lightly-salted water for 45 minutes to 1 hour. Allow to cool completely before adding to the salad.
2 Chop the pepper.
3 Turn the beans, cabbage and mustard and cress in a bowl with the French dressing and the pulped garlic until mixed. Sprinkle with chopped red pepper and serve.

Stuffed Eggs

4 eggs
1 oz (30g) butter
½ teaspoon sea salt
½ teaspoon cayenne pepper
Juice of ½ lemon
1 tablespoon grated cheese
2 oz (55g) black olives
1 tablespoon parsley, chopped
1 tablespoon pimentoes
4 slices wholemeal bread

1 Hard boil the eggs and when quite cool cut in half lengthways.
2 Remove the yolk and pound with butter, salt, cayenne pepper, lemon juice, grated cheese, and the stoned and finely chopped olives.
3 Pile back into the whites and decorate with a little chopped parsley and pimentoes.
4 Serve on a croûton of toast spread with the left-over filling.

7.
VEGETABLES

Stuffed Cabbage Leaves

The stuffing for this recipe is the Basic Savoury Nut Mixture on page 59 or the Chestnut Roast on page 60.

1 large cabbage
2 cups savoury nut mixture
1 onion, chopped
2 tablespoons vegetable oil
1 pint (570ml) vegetable stock

1 Remove the coarse and damaged outer leaves from a cabbage, then select some good leaves, allowing one or two per person.
2 Steam the leaves for 5 minutes then place 2 to 3 tablespoons of nut stuffing into the middle of the leaf, roll up and arrange in a casserole with the folded side downwards.
3 Fry the onion in the oil and spread over the cabbage rolls. Add the vegetable stock to a depth of about 1 inch (2.5cm). Place a lid on the casserole and bake for 1 hour at 350°F/180°C (Gas Mark 4).

Crunchy Chinese Cabbage

1 onion
1 small head of Chinese leaves
1 tablespoon vegetable oil or butter
2 oz (55g) sunflower seeds
1 teaspoon cumin seeds
Sea salt and tamari to taste

1 Slice the onion and Chinese leaves finely and fry in a pan with the oil or butter and the two types of seeds.
2 When the cabbage has softened, sprinkle with sea salt and tamari and serve.

Dolmades (Cabbage Rolls Stuffed with Rice)

2 medium onions
2 oz (55g) mushrooms
2 tablespoons vegetable oil
1 cup cooked brown rice
2 tablespoons chopped nuts
Sea salt and freshly ground black pepper
Pinch freshly ground nutmeg
2 tablespoons grated cheese
1 small savoy cabbage
2 tomatoes, sliced
½ pint (285ml) vegetable stock

1 To prepare the stuffing chop one of the onions and all the mushrooms and fry in the oil. After a few minutes stir in the rice, chopped nuts and seasonings.
2 Remove from the heat and spoon in the grated cheese, mixing well.
3 To prepare the cabbage cut off the stem and peel off the leaves intact. Place in boiling water for a few minutes to soften, then lay the leaves out and divide the stuffing.
4 Roll each leaf around the stuffing and place in the bottom of an oiled casserole.
5 Slice the remaining onion and fry for a few minutes. When soft lay over the cabbage rolls together with slices of tomato.
6 Pour the stock into the casserole and cover with a lid or foil. Bake for 30 minutes at 350°F/180°C (Gas Mark 4). Serve with apple sauce or sweet pickles.

Fried Cabbage and Nuts

The essence of this dish is slow gentle cooking for 10 to 15 minutes. Steam is released from the vegetables so they are part steamed, part fried. The cabbage emerges green and succulent.

1 oz (30g) butter or vegetable oil
1 medium cabbage or other greens
1 onion
1 cup hazelnuts or peanuts
Sea salt and freshly ground black pepper
1 clove garlic

1 Heat the butter or oil in a pan which can be covered closely with a lid or plate.
2 Shred the cabbage and onion with a sharp knife and place in the pan with the nuts chopped or whole. Cover and cook gently for about 15 minutes.
3 Season with a little fresh ground pepper and sea salt and a touch of garlic.

Note: As a variation try adding fresh peas and broad beans, finely sliced sticks of carrot, sweetcorn, or luscious chunks of tomato, but add the last halfway through cooking to prevent them going mushy. Vegetables such as carrots need to be cut fairly finely if they are to be cooked in the same way as cabbage.

Battered Brussels

A mouthwatering combination of Brussels sprouts coated in crisp batter.

4 tablespoons wholemeal flour
½ teaspoon sea salt
1 egg
½ pint (285ml) milk
1 lb (455g) Brussels sprouts
Vegetable oil for deep frying
Juice of 1 lemon

1 To make the batter, sift the flour and salt into a mixing bowl and make a well in the centre. Beat the egg and add to the flour, mixing thoroughly.
2 Add milk until a stiff batter is formed and leave to stand in a cool place for half an hour.
3 Lightly steam or boil the sprouts. When soft, but before they go mushy, roll in flour then coat in batter and fry in deep fat until golden. Serve with a squeeze of lemon juice.

Note: The same treatment can be given to cauliflower florets, slivers of carrot, parsnip and turnip, and sprigs of kale, watercress and young spinach, which should be given only very brief cooking in very hot oil.

Greens au Gratin

½ oz (15g) butter
1 tablespoon wholemeal flour
½ pint (285ml) milk or single cream
Sea salt and freshly ground black pepper
3 oz (85g) Cheddar cheese, grated
1½ lbs (680g) greens, cooked

1 Heat the butter in a pan and stir in the flour, blending thoroughly.
2 Pour in the milk or cream little by little, stirring all the time and add the seasoning. Bring to the boil and cook for 5 minutes, stirring to prevent lumps forming.
3 Remove from the heat and add any further seasoning as necessary. A touch of fresh ground nutmeg gives a fine flavour. Stir in the grated cheese until thoroughly blended in.
4 Pour the sauce over the greens and serve straight away.

Note: This recipe can be used with almost any cooked vegetable.

Seakale with Beans and Mushrooms

1 lb (455g) seakale beet
2 oz (55g) mushrooms
1 cup broad beans (fresh or frozen)
1 oz (30g) butter or vegetable oil
1 sprig peppermint
Sea salt and freshly ground black pepper

1 Remove the midribs from the seakale, cut into half-inch (1.5cm) pieces and sauté with the chopped mushrooms and broad beans in a pan with the oil. Cover with a closely-fitting lid, and after 5 minutes add the rest of the seakale, shredded.
2 Cook over a low heat for 10 more minutes when all should be tender.
3 Chop the peppermint and sprinkle over the completed dish together with a little sea salt and freshly ground pepper.

Beans with Tomato Sauce

This recipe is applicable to French or green beans, young broad beans still in their pods, or hulled broad beans.

1 clove garlic
2 tablespoons vegetable oil
1 lb (455g) fresh tomatoes or 1 large tin
½ teaspoon finely chopped thyme
Sea salt and freshly ground black pepper
1 teaspoon honey
1 lb (455g) fresh peas or beans
1 oz (30g) butter

1 Sauté the sliced or crushed garlic in the oil in a saucepan until it begins to brown.
2 Add the peeled sliced tomatoes and cook gently over a low heat for 15 minutes, adding the thyme towards the end. Season with pepper and salt and add the honey.
3 Prepare and steam the peas or beans and when they are just cooked drain off the water and toss in butter in the pan.
4 Pour over the tomato sauce which may first be sieved or liquidized, and serve immediately.

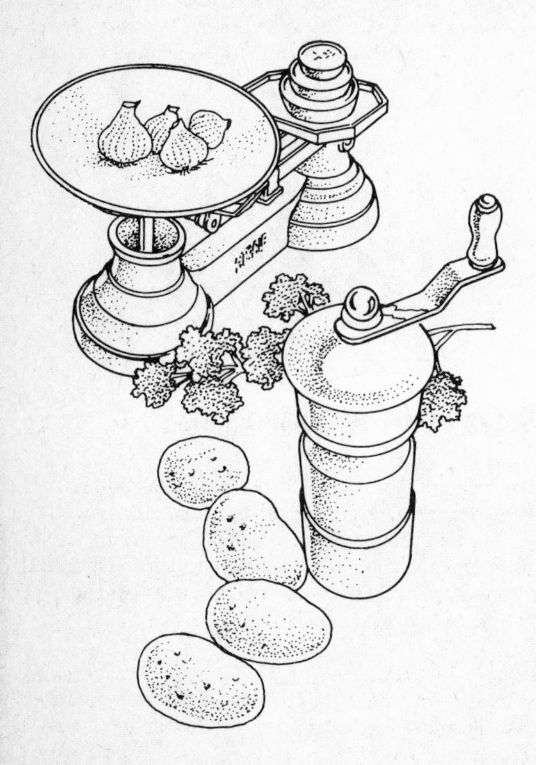

Sautéed Lettuce

Choose a firm head of lettuce and cut into quarters. Cook in a little vegetable oil over a low heat in a covered saucepan. Turn frequently and after 5 minutes sprinkle with a little salt and some tamari. Chopped herbs and nuts may also be added. Can be served with nut rissoles and grilled tomatoes.

French or Green Beans with Cheese

This is really a sensational combination.

1 lb (455g) French or green beans
1 oz (30g) butter
½ clove garlic
¼ teaspoon sea salt
4 oz (115g) grated Cheddar cheese

1 To prepare the beans, cut into short lengths and steam for 10 minutes or until soft.
2 Mix the melted butter, crushed garlic and a little salt on a serving dish.
3 When the beans are cooked toss them in the butter mixture. Sprinkle over the cheese and stir to distribute evenly. Serve immediately.

Stuffed Peppers

4 large green peppers
1 onion
2 tablespoons vegetable oil
2 cups brown rice, cooked
½ cup vegetable stock
2 teaspoons yeast extract
2 tablespoons tomato purée
1 clove garlic
Sea salt and freshly ground black pepper
1 tablespoon oregano

1 Select large perfect peppers. Wash, slice off the tops and remove all the seeds.
2 To prepare the stuffing, chop and fry the onion lightly in the oil. Add the cooked rice and pour in a little stock or water.
3 Stir in the yeast extract, tomato purée (paste) and sliced garlic. Season well and sprinkle with oregano.
4 Stuff the peppers with the rice mixture and replace the tops. Place in an oven dish with a little water to prevent sticking. Bake for 45 minutes at 350°F/180°C (Gas Mark 4).

Note: These stuffed peppers are excellent with garlic mayonnaise. Cabbages, tomatoes and globe artichokes can be stuffed in the same manner. The Basic Savoury Nut Mixture (page 59) also makes a good stuffing and can be used alone or mixed with brown rice.

Glazed Carrots and Shallots

Slices of turnip and swede, leeks and small onions are also delicious when cooked in this way.

12 small carrots
12 small shallots
Vegetable stock to cover
Seasoning
3 tablespoons honey
3 tablespoons butter
½ teaspoon chopped parsley

1 Cover the carrots and shallots with the stock and season. Simmer over a low heat until soft.
2 Arrange the vegetables in an oiled casserole.
3 Melt the honey and butter together, stir in the parsley and pour over the vegetables.
4 Bake in a moderate oven, 350°F/180°C (Gas Mark 4) for 20 minutes.

New Potatoes with Almonds

1½ lbs (680g) new potatoes
2 oz (55g) butter
4 oz (115g) blanched almonds
2 tablespoons parsley, chopped

1 Choose small to medium-sized potatoes and scrub to remove the skin.
2 Melt the butter in a pan and add the whole nuts, potatoes and parsley. A closely-fitting lid on the pan is essential.
3 Cook over a very gentle heat, turning occasionally, until the potatoes are done, which should take 20 to 30 minutes.

Tomatoes Stuffed with Mushrooms

4 large tomatoes
1 level tablespoon wholemeal breadcrumbs
1 small onion, finely chopped
½ level tablespoon parsley, chopped
6 oz (170g) mushrooms, sliced
1 teaspoon Holbrook's Worcestershire sauce
Sea salt and freshly ground black pepper
2 tablespoons grated cheese

1 Slice off the tops of the tomatoes and scoop out the insides. Turn upside down to drain on absorbent paper.
2 Mix the tomato pulp with the breadcrumbs, onion, parsley, mushrooms and a knob of butter. Season with Worcester sauce, salt and pepper.
3 Mix all these ingredients thoroughly and use to fill the tomatoes.
4 Place on a greased baking tray and bake in a moderately hot oven, 400°F/200°C (Gas Mark 6) for 15-20 minutes. Sprinkle with the grated cheese after about 10 minutes cooking.

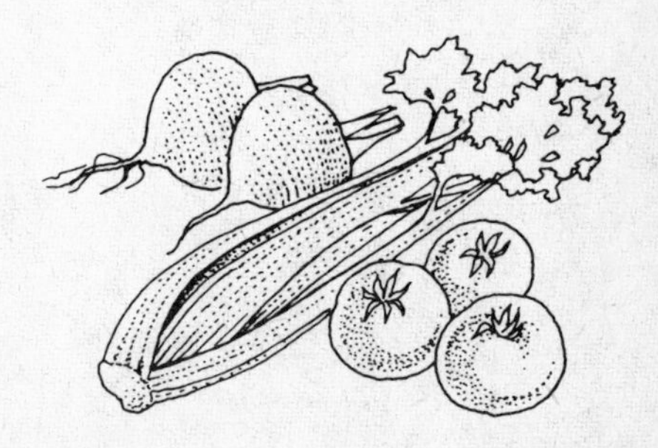

Ways With Mushrooms

Sautéed in Butter
This is perhaps the most delicious plain and simple mushroom recipe. Clean the mushrooms and slice if large. In a heavy skillet melt 2 oz (55g) butter for each ½ lb (225g) mushrooms. Add mushrooms and cook over a gentle heat, stirring frequently. Season with sea salt, freshly ground black pepper and a little lemon juice and serve immediately.

Grilled
Use mushroom cups, or the open type of mushrooms, and grill in a shallow dish, basting with a little melted butter or olive oil.

Baked
Spread the mushrooms out upon a shallow ovenproof dish. Pour a little melted butter on each and sprinkle with fresh wholemeal breadcrumbs and chopped herbs (basil is excellent). Cover tightly with cooking foil and bake in a preheated oven at 375°F/190°C (Gas Mark 5) for 25 minutes. Season with a little salt and pepper and serve.

Stewed in Milk
Place cleaned mushrooms in milk with a pinch of ground mace and cook for 10 minutes or until soft. Drain and pack the mushrooms into a hot serving dish, retaining the milk to make a sauce. In a clean pan melt 1 oz (30g) butter and stir in 1 oz (30g) wholemeal flour for each ½ pint (250ml) milk. When the flour and butter have been cooked together for about a minute begin to add the milk, stirring all the time. Heat and stir until thick and pour over the mushrooms. Before serving pour over a spoonful each of melted butter and redcurrant jelly, and garnish with a sprig of parsley.

Barbecued
Use cleaned mushroom cups. Wrap each in an individual piece of foil, enclosing also a knob of butter, chopped herbs and a dash of tamari. Place near the fire and cook 5 minutes each side.

Cream Sauce with Herbs

This sauce is very good with vegetables, such as asparagus, calabrese, lightly cooked cabbage, spinach etc.

4 oz (115g) butter
4 fl oz (120ml) double cream
1 egg yolk
Sea salt and freshly ground black pepper
Lemon juice
2-4 tablespoons chopped fresh herbs (parsley, tarragon, fennel, dill, basil, or marjoram are all good to start with)

1 Cut up the butter and place in a bowl over a pan of simmering water.
2 When the butter is melted, add the cream and whisk together until blended.
3 Add the egg yolk and continue to whisk until the sauce thickens.
4 Remove the pan from the heat and season the sauce with salt, pepper and lemon juice and add herbs to taste.

8.

MAIN COURSES

Boiled Brown Rice

This is the basic method of cooking brown rice and many of the following recipes use rice cooked in this way.

1 cup brown rice
1½ to 2 cups water
½ teaspoon of sea salt

1 Thoroughly wash the rice in a strainer under the cold tap.
2 Using the above proportions, which may of course be multiplied, place the cold water in a pan with the rice and bring to the boil. Do not add salt at this stage.
3 Reduce the heat and simmer gently, keeping a lid on the pan at all times. Do not stir.
4 After 45 minutes the pan should be dry and the rice just beginning to catch the bottom. This harms neither rice nor pan. Allow to stand for a while and sprinkle with sea salt before using.

Note: Cooked in this way the rice grains should remain intact and separate and have a succulent bite to them. Cooked rice keeps for 4 to 5 days in a cool place, 5 to 7 days in a fridge. For convenience cook a large quantity at the beginning of the week.

Sakura Rice

Before cooking brown rice add one tablespoon of tamari per cup of rice, then proceed as normal. Tamari, or soy sauce, is made by lactic acid fermentation of soya beans, wheat and sea salt and is delicious with rice. Avoid cheaper imitations made with salt, caramel colouring etc.

Fried Rice with Herbs

Rice with a difference, for serving with another dish.

1 onion
2 tablespoons vegetable oil
2 cups cooked brown rice
3 tablespoons fresh herbs, chopped
Sea salt and freshly ground black pepper

1 Cut the onion into thin slices and fry in a little oil until soft.
2 Add the rice, chopped herbs and seasoning. Serve with tamari. For extra colour add two teaspoons of turmeric.

Fried Rice and Vegetables

2 medium onions
1 carrot
2 sticks celery
1 green pepper
3 cups brown rice, cooked
1 tablespoon parsley, chopped
½ tablespoon marjoram, chopped
Sea salt and freshly ground black pepper
2 eggs
Tamari soy sauce

1 Chop the onions, carrot, celery, and pepper and fry in a little oil over a low heat until they soften.
2 Add the cooked rice and fry for a few minutes until thoroughly heated. Add the freshly chopped herbs, and season with freshly ground pepper and sea salt.
3 Break the eggs into the mixture and stir frequently to avoid sticking. When the egg begins to solidify remove from the heat. Serve with a dash of tamari.

Spanish Rice

This makes an attractive side dish for a curry or it can be eaten by itself.

1 large onion
1 clove garlic
2 tablespoons vegetable oil
4 oz (115g) mushrooms
½ cup fresh peas or beans
3 tomatoes
1 tablespoon parsley, chopped
½ tablespoon basil, chopped
Sea salt and freshly ground black pepper
2 oz (55g) black olives
3 cups brown rice, cooked

1 Chop the onion finely and fry with the sliced or pulped garlic in a pan with the oil.
2 When the onion has softened add the chopped mushrooms and peas or beans and cover the pan. Cook for 10 minutes.
3 Add the chopped tomatoes, herbs, seasoning, the stoned quartered olives and lastly rice. Keep turning the mixture until the rice has heated. Serve with tamari.

Mushrooms and Rice

8 oz (225g) mushrooms, chopped
2 tablespoons vegetable oil
Sprig parsley
2 cloves garlic
2 cups brown rice, cooked
Sea salt and freshly ground black pepper

1 Sauté the mushrooms in the oil in a closed pan very slowly until the juices ooze freely.
2 Chop the parsley and garlic finely and add to the pan. Stir in the rice and season.

Basic Omelette

2 eggs
Sea salt and freshly ground black pepper
1 teaspoon butter or vegetable oil

1 Always use fresh eggs and beat well with a fork, at the same time adding the seasoning and any desired herbs.
2 Set the pan heating with 1 teaspoon of oil or preferably butter. When the butter or oil is beginning to smoke pour in the beaten eggs.
3 Keep lifting the edge of the omelette with a fork to allow more liquid from the top to run under and set.
4 Add any filling and continue to cook until the underside begins to brown. If you have used a sufficiently hot pan the omelette should have risen, but if not this can always be achieved by putting under a hot grill for a few moments.
5 When the cooking is finished loosen the edges if stuck, fold in half and slide onto a plate to serve. Garnish with thin slices of tomato, cress, lettuce, herbs etc. and be prepared to serve immediately after cooking.

The entire omelette-making process should take only about 3 minutes so this is an excellent dish for lunchtime snacks. For a very light omelette separate the whites and beat separately until frothy, then fold in the yolks and seasoning and proceed as before.

There are many variations on this basic theme. The following is a selection.

Herb Omelette — Add a tablespoon of finely chopped fresh herbs, such as basil, parsley, thyme, chives, marjoram. A little chopped onion or shallot can also be added.

Cheese Omelette — Gruyère is the best cheese for this purpose, although a strongly flavoured Cheddar is quite suitable. Grate 2 oz (55g) into the centre of the omelette before folding and use plenty of seasoning.

Mushroom and Cream Cheese — Slice and fry a few large mushrooms. Spread a layer of cream cheese over the partially-cooked omelette. Add the mushrooms, with extra seasoning, then fold and cook for one minute more. Try serving with pumpernickel or any rye bread.

Tomato Omelette — Fill the omelette with a layer of very thinly sliced tomatoes sprinkled with sea salt and freshly ground pepper and a good tablespoon of freshly chopped basil. Top with more sliced tomato and a basil leaf.

Rice Omelette

1 onion
1 tablespoon vegetable oil
2 oz (55g) mushrooms
1 cup brown rice, cooked
3 eggs
1 teaspoon butter or vegetable oil
Sea salt and freshly ground black pepper
Tamari

1 To prepare the filling, fry the chopped onion in a little oil until soft. Add the mushrooms and rice and fry for a few more minutes until thoroughly heated, then put aside.
2 Beat the eggs and re-heat the pan with the butter. When the pan is really hot pour in the beaten eggs and, as the bottom layer hardens, keep lifting to allow the liquid to flow beneath.
3 When the egg is nearly set sprinkle with ground pepper and sea salt and add the filling, with a dash of tamari. Fold the omelette and serve.

Note: This is especially good served with spinach tossed in butter, garlic and lemon juice.

Spanish Omelette

Traditionally a large omelette made with 5 or 6 eggs — this recipe serves 4. A Spanish Omelette is ideal for using up cooked potato and any other left-over vegetables. It takes only 5 minutes to cook and it should be served straight away, so have everything else ready prepared, and pre-heat the grill which will be needed for the last stage of cooking.

1 onion, chopped
1 green or red pepper, chopped
1 tablespoon vegetable oil
1 cup cooked vegetables
3-4 medium potatoes, boiled
5 large eggs
3 tablespoons parsley, chopped
Sea salt and freshly ground black pepper

1 Lightly fry the onion and pepper in a little oil until soft and prepare the cooked vegetables and potatoes by dicing or slicing.
2 Heat the pan with a little butter. Beat the eggs and add the chopped parsley and seasoning. Pour half of the eggs into the pan and cook for a minute or two, then add the filling in a layer and cover with the rest of the eggs.
3 Continue to cook under the grill until the eggs have risen and turned golden. Sprinkle with a few chopped chives or other herbs before serving.

Rice with Vegetable Stew

(Serves 2)

1 onion, chopped
1 clove garlic, chopped
2 tablespoons vegetable oil
1 green pepper
2 carrots
4 oz (115g) mushrooms
1 lb (455g) tomatoes, skinned
Sea salt and freshly ground black pepper
1 teaspoon cider vinegar
1 teaspoon yeast extract
1 teaspoon honey
1 tablespoon fresh herbs, chopped
2 cups cooked brown rice, kept hot

1 Fry the onion and garlic in the oil and after a few minutes add the suitably sliced or chopped green pepper, carrots, mushrooms and any other vegetables to hand. Do not add the tomatoes just yet.
2 Cook for 10 minutes, stirring occasionally, then add the tomatoes and season well. Stir in the cider vinegar, yeast extract, honey, and chopped herbs.
3 Cook for a further 20 minutes, or until the vegetables are soft, then adjust seasoning before serving with brown rice.

Basic Curry Sauce

4 tablespoons vegetable oil
2 medium onions
2 cloves garlic
2 chillies
2 cooking apples
1 oz (30g) sultanas
1 oz (30g) wholemeal flour
1-2 tablespoons curry powder
Sea salt and cayenne pepper
1½ pints (850ml) vegetable stock or water
Juice of 1 lime or lemon

1 Heat the oil in a frying pan and add the finely chopped onions and garlic, the sliced chillies and apple, and the sultanas. Cook until the onion begins to brown. Transfer to a saucepan, leaving behind as much oil as possible and put aside.
2 Sprinkle the flour and curry powder into the oil, together with a little salt and cayenne pepper and fry until the colour darkens.
3 Pour in the stock little by little at first, stirring constantly until it thickens and pour over the cooked onion mixture.
4 Simmer with a lid on the pan for 1 hour then add the lime or lemon juice.

Note: This basic curry sauce can now be served as it is, with rice, or it can be incorporated into one of the following curries. It can also be frozen, which is a useful time-saver.

Main Courses

Egg Curry

Basic curry sauce (see page 53)
4 eggs
3 cups brown rice, cooked

1 Whilst the curry sauce is still simmering break the eggs into it and stir until they coagulate into noodle-like strands.
2 Serve with brown rice and dhal (see below).

Bean Curry

1 onion
4 oz (115g) mushrooms
3 carrots
½ oz (15g) butter
2 cups cooked red beans
Basic curry sauce (see page 53)
3 cups brown rice, cooked

1 Cook the finely chopped onion, mushrooms and carrots in the butter until they begin to brown.
2 Add the cooked red beans and pour over the curry sauce and simmer very gently for 10-15 minutes. Serve with brown rice.

Vegetable Curry

2 medium onions
1 carrot
2 sticks celery
1 green pepper
Vegetable oil as necessary
Basic curry sauce (see page 53)
1 tablespoon parsley, chopped
½ tablespoon marjoram
3 cups brown rice, cooked

1 Chop the onions, carrot, celery, and pepper and fry in a little oil over a low heat until they soften.
2 Add the curry sauce and cook gently for a further 15 minutes. Add the freshly chopped herbs, and serve with brown rice.

Dhal

This is an excellent dish to accompany a curry and is always much appreciated. This recipe differs from the traditional Indian version.

½ lb (225g) red lentils
1 onion
2-3 cloves of garlic
2 tablespoons vegetable oil
1 lb (455g) fresh tomatoes (or 1 tin)
2 tablespoons tomato purée
1 oz (30g) butter
Sea salt and freshly ground black pepper

1 Wash the lentils and cook with three times their volume of cold water (no soaking is necessary).
2 Meanwhile prepare a tomato sauce by frying the chopped onion and garlic in the oil, then add the peeled and chopped tomatoes and simmer for 20 minutes. Stir in the tomato purée.
3 When the lentils are cooked they should have absorbed most of the water. The tomato sauce should have thickened, so that when the two are mixed together with the butter the resulting mixture has a fairly thick consistency and is not at all runny.
4 The result should have an intense flavour and if you feel it is not strong enough add a little tomato purée and some more garlic. Season with sea salt and freshly ground pepper to taste and serve.

Curry Side Dishes

Side dishes add variety and when used with imagination can transform a curry into a special meal. Try grated fresh coconut, sliced banana, cucumber in yogurt, finely sliced green peppers, chopped nuts, sliced green apples, nasturtium leaves, cottage cheese with fresh dark cherries, lemon and lime slices, and pickles.

Rice Carrot Casserole

1 oz (30g) butter
1 onion
2 cups brown rice, cooked
2 cups raw shredded carrots
2 eggs
2 teaspoons yeast extract
½ pint (285ml) milk
4 oz (115g) grated Cheddar cheese
1 tablespoon tarragon, chopped

1 Melt the butter in a frying pan and fry in it the finely chopped onion. When soft mix it with the rest of the ingredients in a mixing bowl and turn into an oiled casserole.
2 Stand the casserole in a pan of hot water and bake at 350°F/180°C (Gas Mark 4) for 45 minutes.

Risotto

1 onion, chopped
2 cloves garlic, crushed
2 tablespoons vegetable oil
1 cup brown rice, uncooked
1 tablespoon yeast extract
1 pint (570ml) vegetable stock
2 tablespoons fresh mixed herbs
Sea salt and freshly ground black pepper
4 oz (115g) Cheddar cheese, grated

1 Sauté onion and garlic in oil over a low heat. When soft add the rice and cook for further five minutes, stirring constantly, when the rice should be a golden colour.
2 Dissolve the yeast extract in the stock and sprinkle in the herbs, freshly chopped if available. Season to taste then pour half the stock over the rice.
3 Continue to cook over a low flame, adding more stock as it is absorbed. The rice should be tender in 30 minutes. Stir in half of the cheese and when melted remove from heat, top with the rest of the cheese and serve.

Egg and Mint Pie

Wholemeal pastry, made with ½ lb (225g) wholemeal flour and 4 oz (115g) vegetable margarine (for method see Cheese and Onion Quiche recipe)
1 lb (455g) potatoes, cooked and mashed
4 eggs
Fresh mint

1 Line a well-greased pie dish with half the pastry and cover with a layer of mashed potato.
2 Crack the eggs over the top of this, taking care to keep the yolks intact.
3 Sprinkle liberally with fresh chopped mint and cover with the remaining pastry. Bake for 20 minutes in a moderate oven, 375°F/190°C (Gas Mark 5).

Mushroom and Cheese Puff

(Serves 4 to 6)

4 tablespoons vegetable oil
½ cup chopped onion
1 lb (455g) fresh button mushrooms, wiped and sliced
6 eggs, separated
2 tablespoons grated Parmesan cheese
6 oz (170g) grated Cheddar cheese
2 tablespoons wholemeal flour
2 tablespoons fresh chopped parsley
1 teaspoon sea salt
⅛ teaspoon freshly ground black pepper

1 In a large pan heat the oil and sauté the onions and mushrooms, reserving a few for topping, until golden. Spread evenly over the base of an ovenproof dish and set aside.
2 In a basin beat the egg yolks, then add the cheese, flour, parsley, salt and pepper.
3 Beat the egg whites until stiff peaks are formed.
4 Fold the whites into the cheese mixture and spread this over the mushrooms and onions. Top with reserved sautéed mushrooms.
5 Bake for about 20 minutes in a moderate oven, 350°F/180°C (Gas Mark 4), until puffy and firm.

Cheese and Onion Quiche

3 oz (85g) vegetable margarine
6 oz (170g) wholemeal flour
Sea salt
Ice-cold water
1 onion
4 oz (115g) cheese, grated
3 eggs
½ pint (285ml) milk
1 tablespoon wholemeal flour
2 tablespoons fresh herbs, chopped
Sea salt and freshly ground black pepper
1 large tomato

1 To make the pastry rub the fat into flour and add sea salt to taste. When the mixture is of breadcrumb consistency add a little ice-cold water and knead lightly.
2 Roll out pastry to line a 9-inch (23cm) greased flan tin. Prick the pastry with a fork and bake blind for 10 minutes at 350°F/180°C (Gas Mark 4).
3 Chop and fry the onion in a little vegetable oil until tender and spread in the pre-baked flan case. Cover with the grated cheese.
4 Beat together the eggs, milk, flour, herbs and seasoning, and pour into the flan case. Decorate with slices of tomato before baking.
5 Bake the quiche in the oven for 30 minutes at 375°F/190°C (Gas Mark 5), after which the eggs should be set and the top should be golden brown. Serve with Sakura Rice (see page 51) or Mushrooms and Rice (see page 52) with a salad.

Note: This is equally good served with a salad, or with cooked vegetables such as sprouting broccoli, asparagus, kale, new potatoes etc.

There are many variations you can make from this basic quiche recipe, for example:
Mushroom Quiche — Add 4 oz (115g) mushrooms to the above, chop and fry the mushrooms with the onion.
Leek and Tomato Quiche — Chop 2 medium leeks into short lengths and boil or steam for 10 minutes. With or without the cheese add the leeks with the onion and when the flan is ready to go into the oven top with slices of fresh tomato.
Herb Quiche — Leave out the cheese, replace the milk with single cream, and add 2 extra tablespoons of fresh chopped herbs.
Bean Quiche — Add 1 cup of cooked beans to the onions in the flan case.

Rice Croquettes

These rice croquettes are delicious when served with a salad or cooked vegetables and topped with chutney or pickle.

1 large leek
2 tablespoons vegetable oil
4 oz (115g) grated cheese
2 cups brown rice, cooked
2 tablespoons wholemeal flour
Sea salt and freshly ground black pepper
¼ cup milk
1 egg
Wholemeal breadcrumbs

1 Chop the leek and fry in the vegetable oil until soft.
2 Mix the leeks with the grated cheese, rice, flour and seasoning, adding a little milk to bind if necessary.
3 Form into croquettes and dust with flour. Beat the egg with a little milk and coat the croquettes, then dip in breadcrumbs and fry in oil until crisp.

Pizza Napolitana

Pizza is so easy and is everyone's favourite. It always goes down well, no matter if the weather is hot or cold. Although it is usually made with a special white dough I find that ordinary 100% wholemeal bread dough makes a most acceptable pizza and is very little trouble to make if you save some dough when making bread. This keeps well on a saucer in the fridge for a day or so.

The best cheese to use for pizza is Mozzarella but, failing this, Cheddar will do.

For a special meal add a side dish of fresh salad; a bottle of red wine also goes down well!

¾ lb (340g) bread dough (see page 80)
3 medium onions
2 cloves garlic
2 tablespoons vegetable oil
1½ lbs (680g) fresh, peeled and chopped tomatoes or 1 tin tomatoes
Sea salt and freshly ground black pepper
2 tablespoons fresh chopped oregano
4 oz (115g) black olives
6 oz (170g) cheese, grated

1 Divide the bread dough into two and roll out on a well-floured board, turning often to make sure it doesn't stick. Well oil a large baking sheet and transfer the dough, leaving it in a warm place to rise for about half an hour while you attend to the filling.
2 Take a frying pan and fry the chopped onions and garlic in a little oil. After a few minutes add the tomatoes and cook for a while over a low heat to evaporate some of the juice. Season with salt and pepper.
3 Spread the filling over the dough then sprinkle with oregano and black olives. Cook at the top of a pre-heated oven at 425°F/200°C (Gas Mark 7) for 15 to 20 minutes.
4 Sprinkle on the cheese and return to the oven for a further 5 minutes. Serve straight from the oven.

Spinach and Egg Pie

(Serves 6)

2 onions
2 tablespoons vegetable oil
2 lbs (900g) spinach
4 eggs
⅓ pint (200ml) milk
Sea salt and freshly ground black pepper
4 tablespoons parsley, chopped
4 oz (115g) Cheddar cheese, grated

1 Fry the chopped onions in a little vegetable oil and chop the spinach into small pieces.
2 Beat the eggs with the milk, season with salt and pepper and add the chopped parsley.
3 Mix the onion and spinach and place in an oiled pie dish. Pour over the egg mixture and top with grated cheese. Cook at 375°F/190°C (Gas Mark 5) for 30 to 40 minutes, when the top should be brown and the inside set. Serve with tomatoes, peas or other vegetables.

Baked Lentil Pie

¾ lb (340g) lentils (any type), soaked
½ lb (225g) potatoes
½ oz (15g) butter
¼ cup milk
Sea salt and freshly ground black pepper
1 onion
1 lb (455g) tomatoes
4 tablespoons vegetable oil

1 Cook the soaked lentils until soft and strain off any excess water.
2 Boil the potatoes and when cooked mash with the butter, a little milk, and seasoning.
3 Gently cook the chopped onion and peeled, sliced tomatoes in the vegetable oil until soft.
4 Put the lentils in the bottom of a well-greased casserole then add the onions and tomatoes and for the final layer spread over the mashed potato.
5 Bake for 30 minutes at 375°F/190°C (Gas Mark 5). Serve with lightly steamed green vegetables.

Mixed Bean Stew

The times indicated are suitable for any bean which cooks fairly quickly. For example, aduki beans, brown lentils, black-eyed beans, split peas, red kidney beans, butter beans, haricot beans and borlotti beans, all of which must have been soaked beforehand. Reduce the times by at least half when using a pressure cooker.

1 large onion
2 cloves garlic
4 oz (115g) mushrooms
4 tablespoons vegetable oil
2 pints (1.1 litres) vegetable stock
4 oz (115g) mixed beans
3 large carrots
3 large potatoes
½ small swede
2 Jerusalem artichokes (optional)
2 teaspoons yeast extract
1 teaspoon chopped thyme
Sea salt and freshly ground black pepper
2 tablespoons wholemeal flour

1 Sauté the chopped onions, garlic and mushrooms in the oil and when cooked add the vegetable stock and the soaked beans.
2 Cook for 35 minutes and then add the prepared and diced remaining vegetables and all other ingredients except for the flour.
3 Cook for another 35 minutes or until the vegetables and beans are cooked.
4 Add any further seasoning that may be required and thicken with the flour, first mixing the flour with a little of the liquid from the stew in a cup. When it is lump-free mix into the stew and bring to the boil, stirring until thickening has occurred.

Red Hot Beans!

(Serves 6)

This is a very satisfying but meatless version of Chilli con Carne.

¾ lb (340g) red kidney beans
2 onions, chopped
Vegetable oil as necessary
2-3 large aubergines
1 lb (455g) tomatoes, chopped
Sea salt and freshly ground black pepper
2 cloves garlic
1 teaspoon ground coriander
Chilli powder to taste

1 Soak the beans overnight and cook for 1½ hours, or 30 minutes in a pressure cooker.
2 Fry the onions in the oil in a heavy iron pan and when soft add the diced aubergine. The aubergines will soak up the oil, so keep adding more as they do so.
3 When the aubergines are soft add the tomatoes, salt, pepper, garlic and spices. Start with a very small amount of chilli powder, enough to cover the tip of a knife.
4 After 15 minutes cooking add the cooked beans and simmer for a further 30 minutes over a very gentle heat. Add more chilli powder to taste, but be careful, there is nothing you can do if too much is added — except sweat it out!
Serve with rice.

Lentil Roast

The mixture described below may either be roasted in an ovenproof dish or used to form rissoles which can be fried. Any type of cooked bean may be substituted for the lentils.

Lentil roast is good served with roast potatoes and green vegetables, or it can be left to cool and served in slices. Cold leftover slices can be fried.

½ lb (225g) red lentils
2 onions
1 clove garlic
2 tablespoons vegetable oil
2 cups wholemeal breadcrumbs
1 tablespoon parsley, chopped
½ teaspoon sage, chopped
1 teaspoon thyme, chopped
Sea salt and freshly ground black pepper
2 eggs
4 oz (115g) grated Cheddar cheese

1 Cook the lentils in three times their own volume of water, which should take about 15 minutes.
2 Fry the chopped onion and garlic in the oil and when cooked add to the breadcrumbs in a mixing bowl. Add the chopped herbs and seasoning and mix.
3 Finally add the eggs, the grated cheese and the cooked lentils and mix thoroughly. Place in a well-greased tin and cook in a cool oven, 325°F/170°C (Gas Mark 3) for 40 minutes or until firm.

Main Courses

Mushroom Harvest Pie

For this pie you can use either the pastry recipe given here or ready-made puff pastry.

4 oz (115g) vegetable margarine
½ lb (225g) wholemeal flour
Sea salt and freshly ground black pepper
Ice-cold water
1 medium potato
1 medium onion
2 medium-sized carrots
½ lb (225g) leeks
2 oz (55g) butter
½ lb (225g) button mushrooms
Milk, as necessary
1 oz (30g) wholemeal flour
4 oz (115g) cheese, grated

1. To make the pastry, rub the fat into the flour and add seasoning to taste. When the mixture is of breadcrumb consistency add a little ice-cold water and knead lightly. Chill the dough until it is needed.
2. Thinly slice the potato, onion and carrots and trim, wash and slice the leeks.
3. Melt half the butter in a pan and fry the onion and leeks for 5 minutes or until soft.
4. Add the carrots, potato and ½ pint (285ml) water. Bring to the boil and simmer until the vegetables are cooked. Drain and reserve the stock.
5. Put the cooked vegetables into a 2-pint (1.1 litre) dish. Wipe the mushrooms and put them in also.
6. Make the reserved stock up to ½ pint (285ml) with milk.
7. Melt the remaining butter in a pan, add the flour and cook for one minute. Stir in the vegetable-milk stock and bring to the boil. Cook for 2 minutes, stirring continuously.
8. Add half the grated cheese and season well. Pour over the vegetables in the dish.
9. Roll out the pastry and use to cover the pie dish. Seal the edges and decorate.
10. Bake in a hot oven, 425°F/220°C (Gas Mark 7), for 20 minutes. Sprinkle remaining cheese over the pie and cook for a further 10 minutes.

Savoury Lentils

½ lb (225g) green or brown lentils
1 pint (570ml) vegetable stock
1 onion
2 tablespoons vegetable oil
1 tablespoon wholemeal flour
Juice of 1 lemon

1. Soak the lentils overnight in the stock then cook in the same liquid until tender, adding more stock if required. After about 30 minutes the lentils should be soft but not mushy and can be drained and set aside.
2. Sauté the sliced onion in the oil then mix with the lentils and the flour in a bowl. Dress with the lemon juice and serve.

Spaghetti with Aduki Beans

This is spaghetti served with a basic tomato sauce. The beans add flavour and protein and turn this into a most satisfying meal. The fresh tomatoes can be replaced by a large tin when out of season. A teaspoon or so of tomato purée may also be needed, depending on the flavour of the tomatoes. The aim is to have the pasta and sauce ready at the same time. While the sauce will not be harmed by cooling and re-heating, the pasta should be served the minute it is ready.

1 large onion
2 cloves garlic
2 tablespoons vegetable oil
2 lbs (900g) ripe tomatoes
1 cup cooked aduki beans
Sea salt and freshly ground black pepper
½-¾ lb (225-340g) wholemeal spaghetti
1 oz (30g) butter
2 tablespoons parsley, chopped
2 oz (55g) grated cheese

1. To make the sauce, chop the onion and garlic and fry in the oil until soft.
2. Add the peeled and chopped tomatoes and continue to cook very gently until some of the juice has been given off and the sauce begins to thicken. This should take 15 to 25 minutes.
3. Add the pre-cooked aduki beans and cook for another 10 minutes, then season with sea salt and pepper.
4. To cook the pasta bring a large pan of boiling water to the boil. Add the pasta and stir frequently to discourage sticking. Cooking time will take from 10 to 15 minutes and should leave the pasta soft, but not soggy.
5. Turn the pasta into a colander and leave for at least 2 minutes to drain.
6. Place the butter and some crushed garlic in a serving bowl and put to warm in the oven. Transfer the pasta and stir in the chopped parsley and grated cheese. The bean and tomato sauce may now be poured over, or served separately.

Vegetable Lasagne

(Serves 8-10)

1 lb (455g) onions, sliced
1 lb (455g) carrots, diced
1 head celery, chopped
8 tablespoons vegetable oil
1×15 oz (425g) tin tomatoes
1½ lbs (680g) mushrooms, sliced
1 teaspoon mixed herbs
Sea salt and freshly ground black pepper
½ lb (225g) wholemeal lasagne pasta
3 oz (85g) butter
3 oz (85g) wholemeal flour
2 pints (1.1 litres) milk
1 bay leaf
¾ lb (340g) cheese, grated

1 Sauté the onions, carrots and celery in the oil for 10 minutes.
2 Add the tomatoes and mushrooms, with herbs and seasoning, and cook for a further 15 minutes on a medium heat.
3 Cook the lasagne, adding the pasta strips to a large pan of boiling salted water, simmering for 10-15 minutes.
4 Melt the butter in a pan, add the flour and cook for 2 minutes. Stir in the milk and heat until thickened. Add the bay leaf and leave to stand for 10 minutes, covering the pan with a lid. Then add half of the cheese to the sauce and stir well.
5 Arrange a layer of the vegetable mixture at the bottom of a large ovenproof dish, cover with a layer of the pasta and add one-third of the cheese sauce. Repeat until 3 layers have been completed, then top with the remaining cheese.
6 Bake in a pre-heated oven, 350°F/180°C (Gas Mark 4) for about 1¼ hours or until the top is golden and bubbling.

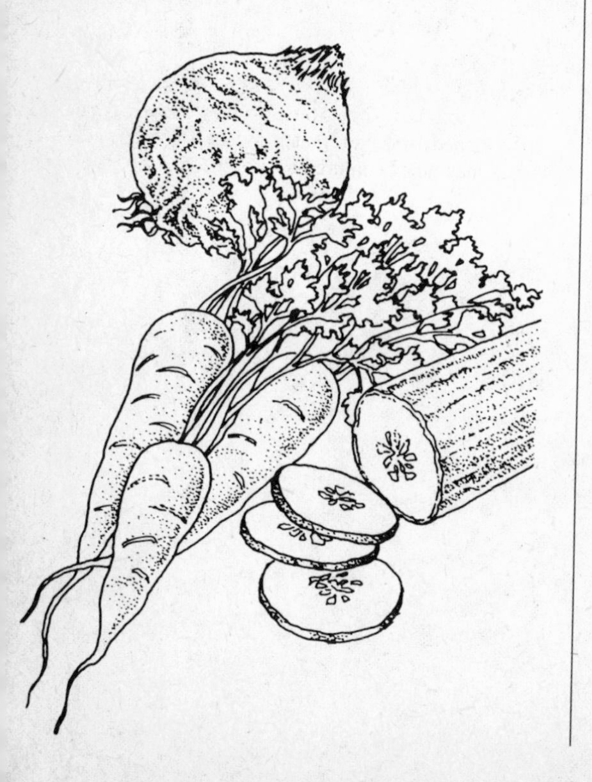

Basic Savoury Nut Mixture

This basic mixture can be cooked in a number of ways and, with various additions, can be incorporated into a variety of recipes. Almost any nuts can be used. The recipes which follow suggest ways of using this basic mixture.

2 medium onions
2 tablespoons vegetable oil
½ lb (225g) nuts
1 cup wholemeal breadcrumbs
1 tablespoon parsley, chopped
1 tablespoon thyme, chopped
Sea salt and freshly ground black pepper
1 oz (30g) vegetable margarine
2 eggs
1 tablespoon tomato purée

1 Chop the onions and fry in a little vegetable oil, but do not allow to brown.
2 Put the nuts through a mincer or briefly liquidize. The idea is to chop them into small pieces without reducing them to paste.
3 Add the nuts to the breadcrumbs in a mixing bowl and stir in the chopped herbs, salt and pepper. Now add the cooked onion and rub in the margarine.
4 Mix in the two eggs, which should bind the ingredients and give a workable consistency. Add a little water if necessary.

Nut Loaf

Place the basic mixture into a well-greased bread tin and bake in a moderately hot oven 375°F/190°C (Gas Mark 5) until brown on top, which should take about 30 minutes. Can be topped with a few nuts before baking.

Nut Rissoles

Form into fritters, coat in dry wholemeal breadcrumbs and fry gently in vegetable oil, turning to brown both sides. These rissoles make a very satisfying accompaniment to a salad or to any cooked vegetable dish. They can also be eaten cold with a packed meal.

Nut Balls

Form into balls about one-inch (2.5cm) in diameter and deep fry. They make an appetizing snack or starter, or can be used with other dishes or salads. Nut Balls are also excellent for use in place of meat balls for a vegetarian spaghetti bolognese.

Potato and Nut Cakes

Mash cooked potatoes with butter, salt and pepper. Blend equal quantities of nut mixture and mashed potato and form into cakes about ½ inch (1.5cm) thick. Roll in wholemeal breadcrumbs and fry gently until brown on both sides.

Nut Sausages

For sausages a smooth mixture is essential, so make sure the nuts are very well chopped and the breadcrumbs finely minced. The seasoning should include plenty of pepper and sage. Although the mixture can be rolled into shape, an icing bag without the nozzle produces a better result. Fry and serve in the normal way.

Chestnut Roast

This can be roasted and eaten separately or used as chestnut stuffing.

2 cups cooked chestnuts, or tinned purée
1 cup wholemeal breadcrumbs
2 tablespoons parsley, chopped
½ tablespoon thyme, chopped
Sea salt and freshly ground black pepper
1 medium onion
2 tablespoons vegetable oil
1 egg

1 Skin the chestnuts by oiling their skins, slitting, and baking in a moderate oven for 15 to 20 minutes.
2 Mash thoroughly then mix with the breadcrumbs, chopped herbs and seasoning.
3 Fry the finely chopped onion in some vegetable oil and add to the mixture. Break in the egg and mix well.
4 Bake in a well-oiled tin at 375°F/190°C (Gas Mark 5) for about 30 minutes or until brown on top.

9.

BARBECUE MEALS

Introduction

Although the conventional barbecue meal is centred around meat there is no need for vegetarians to forgo the social and gastronomic pleasures of eating barbecued food.

Barbecues are one of the easiest and most relaxing ways of entertaining and make much more of an 'event' than an ordinary meal. They are popular with adults and children alike and are ideal for parties and celebrations. Their use for normal family meals should not be neglected and, in the warmer months, a barbecue lunch or evening meal out in the fresh air can be very enjoyable. Whatever the event, the cook is not banished to the kitchen while the meal is being prepared. In fact, family or guests will probably be eager to lend a hand.

Don't be put off by the expensive barbecues displayed in shops and garden centres. If you find you are regularly eating barbecue meals you may like to splash out on one of these, but to begin with you can manage with a bag of charcoal and a few bricks, or one of the very cheap Japanese 'hibachi' type barbecues. The essence of barbecue cookery is simplicity and, to my mind, this is the way it should be kept. Use the best of fresh and wholesome ingredients and do not feel you have to follow the recipes to the letter. Use them as a basis for your own ideas.

Utensils and Accessories

A good pair of tongs are indispensible for moving about the hot coals and manipulating the food. A sturdy long-handled pair will serve you best. Next in usefulness comes a long-handled fork. A wok with lid is the ideal type of pan to use on a barbecue for all types of cooking. Thick aluminium foil is also indispensible for the vegetarian barbecue as vegetables need to retain their moisture for successful cooking and do not respond in the same way as meat to cooking by radiant heat. Brushes are needed for basting food while it is cooking, preferably the bristle type rather than nylon which melts easily.

To keep the fire in order a poker is useful and for maintaining a good draught an ash scraper would be useful. After use, a thorough brushing with a stiff wire brush is all that's needed to keep your barbecue in good and clean condition. Kebab skewers do not have to skewer meat — they can be used to cook all manner of vegetable delights. A pair of oven gloves are also a good idea especially for removing foil from cooked food. A trolley or table standing near the grill with everything to hand will make life a lot simpler for the cook.

Wooden bowls, boards and plates are particularly good for serving food out of doors as they are unbreakable and do not cool the food unduly. Never soak wood ware. Simply wipe clean with a damp cloth and rub in a little olive oil to seal the wood. After a while they develop a rich and beautiful patina. Plastic utensils have the same advantages but are less appealing to use and deteriorate more rapidly, especially around a hot fire.

Burgers and Sausages

In the traditional barbecue, burgers and sausages form a large part of the menu. These pleasures need not be denied the vegetarian as there are many meatless substitutes which can be bought or made at home. Although some purists may dismiss these on the basis that they are a meat imitation, my own feeling is that burgers and sausages have the least 'meaty' characteristics of any of the carnivorous foods and that they provide a substitute not for meat itself but for a texture which can be lacking in vegetarian food.

Frozen vegetarian burgers are now widely available and are very convenient, although I personally prefer some of the other dry mixes such as *Sosmix,* which I think have a better flavour and texture and which can be modified during the mixing. I like to add herbs, fried onions, freshly ground black pepper and sometimes a little crushed garlic to improve the flavour.

Serving Suggestions

As with most vegetarian foods, every part of the traditional hamburger can be improved upon to such an extent that even hardened meat eaters will actually prefer them. For a start, wholemeal rolls have a far more interesting flavour and texture. Some very good wholemeal rolls are available these days, and most bakeries have a selection. I like particularly the 'Turkestan' rolls which have a moist, grainy texture and are topped with crunchy cracked wheat and sesame seeds. If you prefer to make your own rolls there is a recipe on page 64.

Home-made or good quality bought relishes and chutneys can add the finishing touch to a really succulent barbecue hamburger. Most supermarkets now carry a range of relishes including barbecue relish, tomato, onion, cucumber, sweetcorn and others.

Burger and Sausage Mixes

The recipes which follow will all need preparation beforehand but, once formed into burgers or sausages, they freeze well, which can be a useful time saver. Just lay them out on trays until frozen and, when hard, store in sealed bags. Allow not less than 15 minutes to defrost before cooking on the grill over hot charcoal. Turn several times until done.

For sausages, a uniform mixture is essential, so make sure that beans are well mashed or nuts, if used, are very finely chopped. Breadcrumbs should be minced or liquidized. Use plenty of seasoning including freshly ground black pepper and herbs such as thyme and sage. Although the mixture can be rolled into shape, an icing bag without the nozzle produces a better result.

Lentil or Bean Burger Mix

½ lb (225g) red lentils
2 onions, chopped
1 clove garlic
2 tablespoons vegetable oil
2 cups wholemeal breadcrumbs
1 tablespoon parsley, chopped
1 teaspoon sage, chopped
1 teaspoon thyme, chopped
Sea salt and freshly ground black pepper
2 eggs
4 oz (115g) Cheddar cheese, grated

1 Cook the lentils in three times their own volume of water, which should take about 15 minutes.
2 Fry the chopped onion and garlic in the oil and, when cooked, add to the breadcrumbs in a mixing bowl.
3 Add the chopped herbs, salt and pepper, then mix.
4 Finally add the eggs, the grated cheese and the cooked lentils and mix thoroughly. If the mixture will not form into burgers add a few more breadcrumbs to dry it a little.

Note: Any type of cooked bean may be substituted for the lentils.

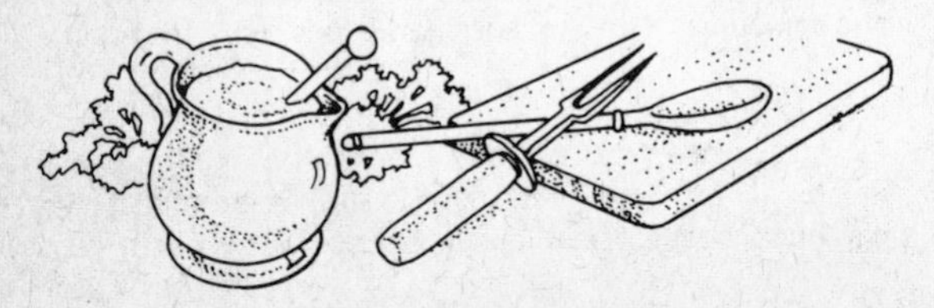

Barbecue Bean Burger Mix

½ lb (225g) soaked red kidney beans (or 1 tin red kidney beans)
2 large onions, chopped
1½ oz (40g) butter
4 tablespoons parsley, chopped
2 oz (55g) wholemeal flour
2 oz (55g) wholemeal breadcrumbs
1 tablespoon soya sauce
1 tablespoon tomato purée

1 Leave the beans to soak overnight.
2 Next day boil in a large pan with plenty of water (and no salt).
3 While the beans are cooking, sauté the onion in the butter until soft.
4 When the beans are cooked, which will take at least 30 minutes, strain in a colander then mash.
5 Stir in the cooked onions and the rest of the ingredients and leave to cool.
6 Roll out on a floured board and cut into rounds with a large tumbler or biscuit cutter to form into burgers.
7 Grill, basting with butter or oil, until crisp on both sides and serve.

Vegetable Burger Mix

2 medium onions
1 clove garlic
1 tablespoon butter
1 tablespoon vegetable oil
1 large aubergine
4 oz (115g) mushrooms
15 oz (425g) tin tomatoes
1 teaspoon fresh thyme, chopped
Sea salt
Freshly ground black pepper
4 oz (115g) red lentils
4 oz (115g) wholemeal breadcrumbs

1 Thinly slice the onion and garlic and sauté in the butter and oil until soft.
2 Chop the aubergine and mushrooms and add to the onion.
3 Add the tomatoes, herbs and seasonings and simmer gently for 15 minutes so that some of the juice evaporates.
4 In a separate pan cook the lentils for 15 minutes, by which time all the water should have been absorbed.
5 Stir in the lentils and breadcrumbs and leave to stand for 5 minutes.
6 Form into burgers and grill, basting with oil or butter, until nicely browned on both sides.

Mushroom Burger Mix

2 medium onions
1 green pepper
1 oz (30g) butter
½ lb (225g) mushrooms
4 oz (115g) wholemeal breadcrumbs
2 eggs
Sea salt
Freshly ground black pepper
1 teaspoon mixed herbs

1 Chop the onion and green pepper finely and fry in the butter until soft.
2 Chop half of the mushrooms finely and fry with the pepper and onion for a minute or two.
3 Remove from the heat and add the breadcrumbs and the eggs.
4 Mix well and season to taste with sea salt, freshly ground pepper and herbs.
5 Form into burgers or sausages and grill.
6 Slice the remainder of the mushrooms and fry in butter until brown.
7 Serve the burgers topped with mushrooms on a plate or in a hamburger roll.

Chestnut Burger Mix

2 cups chestnut purée
1 cup wholemeal breadcrumbs
1 tablespoon thyme, chopped
½ tablespoon sage, chopped
Sea salt and freshly ground black pepper
1 medium onion, finely chopped
2 tablespoons vegetable oil
1 egg

1 Mash the chestnut purée with the breadcrumbs, chopped herbs and seasoning.
2 Fry the finely chopped onion in vegetable oil and add to the mixture.
3 Break in the egg and mix well.
4 Form into burgers or sausages on a floured board, brush with oil and grill.

Peanut Burger Mix

2 medium onions
2 tablespoons vegetable oil
½ lb (225g) peanuts
1 cup wholemeal breadcrumbs
1 tablespoon parsley, chopped
1 teaspoon thyme, chopped
Sea salt and freshly ground black pepper
1 oz (30g) vegetable margarine
2 eggs
1 tablespoon tomato purée

1 Chop the onions and fry in a little vegetable oil, but do not allow to brown.
2 Put the nuts through a mincer or liquidize briefly. The idea is to chop them into small pieces without reducing them to paste.
3 Add the nuts to the breadcrumbs in a mixing bowl and stir in the chopped herbs, salt and pepper. Now add the cooked onion and rub in the margarine.
4 Mix in the two eggs which should bind the ingredients and give a workable consistency. Add the tomato purée and a little water if necessary.
5 Form into burgers and grill until browned on both sides.

Potato and Nut Burgers

½ lb (225g) potatoes
2 tablespoons butter
1 medium onion
4 oz (115g) mushrooms
2 tablespoons vegetable oil
Sea salt
Freshly ground black pepper
1 tablespoon parsley, chopped
3 oz (85g) chopped almonds or other nuts

1 Peel and boil the potatoes and, when cooked, mash with the butter.
2 While the potato is cooking, slice the onions and mushrooms and sauté in the oil.
3 Season the mashed potato and stir in the parsley, cooked onion, mushrooms and chopped nuts.
4 Form into burgers.
5 Brush with oil and grill.

Rice Burgers

1 onion, chopped
2 tablespoons oil
4 oz (115g) brown rice, cooked
2 tablespoons wholemeal breadcrumbs
2 oz (55g) Cheddar cheese, grated
1 tablespoon 81 per cent wholemeal self-raising flour
1 egg
½ tablespoon tomato purée
Sea salt
Freshly ground black pepper

1 Fry the chopped onion in the oil.
2 When soft mix with the rice, breadcrumbs, grated cheese, flour, egg, tomato purée and seasonings to form a thick dough.
3 Form into burgers or sausages.
4 Brush with vegetable oil and grill or fry over charcoal, turning until both sides are golden brown.
5 Serve with wholemeal rolls and relish.

Dry Mix for Burgers

Make up this dry mix and keep in a jar for immediate use at short notice.

2 oz (55g) hard vegetable fat
2 tablespoons freeze-dried chopped onions
½ lb (225g) peanuts
1 cup wholemeal breadcrumbs
1 teaspoon dried parsley
½ teaspoon dried thyme
Sea salt and freshly ground black pepper

1 Grate the vegetable fat with a medium grater.
2 Mix all the dry ingredients.
3 Stir the fat into the dry ingredients.
4 Store in an airtight jar in a cool place for up to 1 month.
5 To use, stir in enough water to form a stiff dough.
6 Form into burgers and grill.

Cheese Hamburgers

1 small onion, chopped
1 oz (30g) butter
4 oz (115g) cheese, Cheddar or Gruyère
1 lb (455g) burger mix from any one of the previous recipes
1 teaspoon English mustard
6 wholemeal hamburger rolls
Sea salt and freshly ground black pepper

1 Sauté the onion in the butter until soft.
2 Grate the cheese into the burger mix and add the cooked onions and mustard.
3 Form into six burgers and cook over the grill for a few minutes each side until done.
4 Place in the split rolls and serve straight away with pickle or relish.

Salad Hamburgers

Serve your hamburgers between wholemeal rolls with crisp lettuce, watercress and slices of tomato or any other salad ingredient which takes your fancy. Dress with your favourite relish or garlic mayonnaise.

Crunchy Wholemeal Burger Buns

This recipe will make 16 to 20 rolls which can be eaten as soon as they have cooled or may be frozen for future use.

2 oz (55g) whole or cracked wheat grains
2 tablespoons malt extract
¼ pint (140ml) hot water
1 oz (30g) fresh yeast
1½-1¾ pints (850-1000ml) warm water
3 lbs (1.35 kilos) wholemeal flour
1 tablespoon sea salt
2 tablespoons vegetable oil
¼ pint (140ml) milk
2 tablespoons sesame seeds

1 Soak the wheat and malt extract in the hot water for several hours or overnight.
2 Stir the yeast into a cup of the warm water and leave until it begins to froth.
3 Mix the flour and salt in a warmed bowl.
4 Stir into the flour and add the rest of the water, the yeast mixture, and the soaked wheat and malt extract.
5 Knead on a floured board for 10 minutes until a smooth dough is formed.
6 Return to the mixing bowl, cover with a cloth and leave to rise in a warm place for about 1½ hours or until doubled in size.
7 Knead again on a floured board for a few minutes then divide into equal pieces and form into rolls.
8 Lay out on greased trays and decorate the tops by brushing with milk and sprinkling with sesame seeds.
9 Cover and leave to rise again for 20 minutes in a warm place.
10 Bake in a pre-heated oven at 425°F/220°C (Gas Mark 7) for 20-30 minutes.
11 Turn onto wire racks and cool.

Kebabs

Kebabs, like sausages and burgers, are an essential part of any barbecue. Most vegetables can be cooked in this way and can be supplemented by burger mix formed into balls and skewered alongside them. Try whole mushrooms, chunks of onion, pepper, aubergine, tomato, celery and small potatoes. Firmer vegetable such as potatoes and onions can first be softened by blanching in boiling water for a few minutes. Fruits can also be combined with vegetables or burger mixes, in particular pineapple, banana, orange, peaches, figs and mangoes.

Cook kebabs over a medium heat turning frequently. Remember that, with meaty kebabs, the meat supplies the fat for sealing and cooking, but with the vegetarian version you will need to baste occasionally with good quality vegetable oil or butter. To do this, keep a cup of oil or melted butter and a pastry brush handy. Remove the kebab from the grill when basting. Alternatively, you can marinate the vegetables beforehand and baste with some of the marinade during cooking.

Have all the foods you intend to cook prepared beforehand. For a do-it-yourself barbecue you can provide your guests with the skewers and the ingredients in bowls and let them choose and cook their own combinations.

Kebabs can be served as they are or with a sauce or relish.

Basic Vegetable Kebabs

2 large aubergines
½ lb (225g) tiny onions
2 green peppers
½ lb (225g) button mushrooms
6 tomatoes
Vegetable oil
Sea salt and freshly ground black pepper

1 Slice the aubergines into 1-inch (2.5cm) cubes, sprinkle with sea salt and place in a colander to drain for 20 minutes.
2 Rinse the aubergine cubes in cold running water.
3 Meanwhile, skin the onions then cook them with the aubergines for 10 minutes in boiling water.
4 Wash and remove the seeds from the peppers and cut into 1-inch (2.5cm) squares.
5 Wipe the mushrooms clean with a kitchen towel or tissue and halve the tomatoes.
6 Skewer all the vegetables and baste with the oil.
7 Sprinkle with sea salt or garlic salt and freshly ground black pepper and cook over a medium-hot fire.
8 Baste with more oil from time to time and after 15 minutes or so they should be ready to serve.

Mushroom and Tomato Kebabs

½ lb (225g) small tomatoes
½ lb (225g) button mushrooms
4 oz (115g) tiny onions
Basic Marinade (page 66)

1 Peel the tomatoes and cut into quarters.
2 Clean the mushrooms with a kitchen towel and peel the onions.
3 Marinate all the ingredients for 2 hours.
4 Skewer the ingredients and baste with more of the marinade while cooking.

Green Tomato Kebabs

1 clove garlic
½ teaspoon sea salt
¼ pint (140ml) vegetable oil
1 lb (455g) large green tomatoes
4 oz (115g) tiny onions
2 red peppers

1 Skin the garlic and slice thinly with a sharp knife.
2 Sprinkle salt over the garlic and grind to a pulp with the back of a spoon.
3 Mix the garlic pulp into the oil and leave to stand for an hour or so.
4 Wash and slice the green tomatoes thickly.
5 Wash and de-seed the peppers and cut into 1-inch (2.5cm) squares.
6 Skewer and brush with the garlic oil.
7 Baste frequently during cooking with more of the oil.

Fruity Kebabs

4 oz (115g) tiny onions or shallots
1 medium green pepper
½ lb (225g) pineapple cubes, fresh or tinned
2 peaches or 1×7 oz (200g) tin peach slices
1 large orange divided into segments

1 Blanch the skinned onions or shallots in boiling water for 5 minutes.
2 Wash and remove the seeds from the pepper and cut into ¾-inch (2cm) squares.
3 Cut the pineapple into cubes if not already prepared and slice the peaches.
4 Skewer and baste the prepared ingredients with marinade or vegetable oil and cook.

Banana Kebabs

Although the combination of banana, onion and tomato in this recipe sounds rather unlikely it is in fact quite delicious.

4 oz (115g) tiny onions
3 firm bananas
½ lb (225g) small tomatoes
¼ pint (140ml) good quality vegetable oil
2 tablespoons fresh lemon juice
½ tablespoon white wine vinegar
½ teaspoon garlic salt
1 tablespoon chopped basil

1 Skin and blanch the onions by boiling for 5 minutes.
2 Peel and cut the bananas into ½-inch (1cm) slices.
3 Peel the tomatoes by dipping briefly into boiling water then halve.
4 Prepare a marinade by mixing the oil, lemon juice, vinegar, garlic salt and chopped basil.
5 Marinate all the prepared ingredients for 2 hours.
6 Skewer and baste frequently with more of the marinade while cooking.

Basic Marinade for Vegetables

½ pint (285ml) good quality vegetable oil
¼ pint (140ml) white wine vinegar or cider vinegar
Sea salt
Freshly ground black pepper
1 teaspoon soft raw cane sugar

1 Mix all the ingredients together and leave to stand for an hour or so, stirring occasionally until the sugar is dissolved.
2 Pour over the vegetables or fruit before they are skewered and leave to marinate for 2 hours.
3 Skewer the food and cook over a medium grill.
4 Brush the kebabs with the marinade every few minutes until the food is tender.

Marinade with Herbs and Garlic

2 medium cloves garlic
½ teaspoon sea salt
1 cup olive or *walnut oil*
Juice of 2 lemons
Freshly ground black pepper
1 teaspoon soft raw cane sugar
1 tablespoon fresh oregano, chopped (or ½ tablespoon dried)
1 tablespoon fresh basil, chopped (or ½ tablespoon dried)

1 Slice and crush the garlic with the sea salt.
2 Mix the garlic into the oil then add the lemon juice.
3 Season with pepper and then add the sugar.
4 Allow to stand, but stir every few minutes until the sugar has dissolved.
5 Lastly, stir in the fresh chopped herbs. Leave for at least 1 hour before use so that the flavours have time to mingle.
6 Marinate the vegetables following the instructions in the basic recipe (above).

Orange Marinade

½ pint (285ml) cold-pressed olive oil
2½ fl oz (75ml) white wine
¼ pint (140ml) fresh orange juice
Sea salt and freshly ground black pepper
½ teaspoon soft raw cane sugar

1 Beat all the ingredients together with a whisk and leave to stand for an hour or so, stirring occasionally until the sugar is dissolved.
2 To use, marinate the kebab ingredients for at least 2 hours.
3 Skewer the food and cook over a medium grill.
4 Brush with the marinade every few minutes until the food is done.

SAUCES, RELISHES AND EXTRAS

Simple meals are often the most appreciated and, using some of the following recipes, you can transform very simple barbecue meals into something which seems quite special. The various butters can be used in potatoes, on bread, or for basting. Sauces can be used as a dip or poured over barbecue foods, and relishes add a sparkle to even the dullest meal. Garlic bread is always popular, and is useful for mopping up the sauces, or you can try Garlic Rolls or Herb Bread as variations.

Nut Butter

Peanut butter or indeed any nut butter can be made as follows:

½ lb (225g) roasted peanuts
½ cup vegetable oil
1 teaspoon sea salt

1 Liquidize the lightly roasted nuts in a blender, adding good quality vegetable oil little by little until a smooth creamy consistency is obtained.
2 Finally add sea salt to taste. The butter will keep for several weeks in a screw-top jar in the fridge, although it rarely gets the chance.

Note: This is not quite as easy as it sounds because the blender will become clogged and will have to be stopped frequently to free the mixture with a spoon. Don't be tempted to do anything with the blender switched on.

Herb Butter

Use in place of ordinary butter with baked potatoes or with any of the recipes in this book where butter is an ingredient. Use whatever herb or selection of herbs you prefer. Try basil, bay, chervil, chives, dill, garlic, marjoram, parsley, rosemary, sage, tarragon, thyme, lemon balm, mint, summer savory, fennel or lovage. If you prefer margarine, use only good quality soft vegetable margarine. Do not use slimmers' margarine which has a high water content.

4 oz (115g) salted butter or *polyunsaturated vegetable margarine*
3 tablespoons chopped fresh mixed herbs

1 Cream the softened butter or margarine with an electric mixer or by hand using a wooden spoon.
2 Stir in the chopped herbs of your choice.

Lemon and Parsley Butter

This butter is delicious with baked potatoes or as a baste for kebabs.

4 oz (115g) salted butter
Juice of 1 lemon
2 tablespoons fresh parsley, chopped

1 Heat the butter over a low heat until melted and beginning to brown a little.
2 Remove from the heat, pour in the lemon juice and add the parsley.
3 Stir thoroughly, and leave to cool.

Garlic Butter

2 cloves garlic
¼ teaspoon sea salt
4 oz (115g) salted butter
1 tablespoon lemon juice
Freshly ground black pepper

1 Thinly slice the garlic with a sharp knife.
2 Place on a saucer, sprinkle with sea salt and crush together with a spoon.
3 In a bowl, cream the butter with a spoon then add the garlic and lemon juice.
4 Mix thoroughly and add freshly ground pepper to taste.

Horseradish Butter

4 oz (115g) soft butter or polyunsaturated margarine
1 tablespoon prepared mustard
1 teaspoon prepared horseradish
½ teaspoon sea salt
Freshly ground black pepper
1 tablespoon parsley, chopped

1 Combine all the ingredients except the parsley.
2 Cream until thoroughly mixed and light fluffy texture is achieved.
3 Garnish with chopped parsley and serve with corn on the cob or potatoes baked in their jackets.

Tomato Relish

This delicious relish is far better than any bought alternative that I have tasted. It is easy to make and needs no cooking. You will need four 1 lb (500g) jam jars or equivalent.

4 lbs (2.3 kilos) ripe tomatoes
1½ lb (680g) shallots
1 oz (30g) sea salt
3 large sticks celery
1 red pepper
1 lb (455g) Demerara sugar
1 tablespoon mustard seeds
¾ pint (425ml) white wine vinegar

1 Peel the tomatoes by dipping briefly in boiling water.
2 Chop the tomatoes and shallots finely, sprinkle with the salt and leave overnight, or for at least 8 hours.
3 Place the tomatoes and shallots in a sieve and rinse under cold running water, then leave until well drained.
4 Chop the celery and the de-seeded pepper and mix together in a bowl.
5 Add the sugar, mustard seeds, vinegar, and lastly the tomatoes and shallots.
6 Pot into jars, seal, and keep for at least 6 weeks before using.

Sweetcorn Relish

This is a relish you can make yourself the day before the barbecue. Make it as spicy or as mild as you wish.

2 large cooking apples
2 celery sticks
1 red pepper
1 green pepper
4 spring onions
1 small clove garlic
½ lb (225g) sweetcorn, frozen or tinned
2 tablespoons brown sauce
¼ teaspoon sea salt

1 Peel and core the apples and place in a saucepan with just enough water to cover the bottom.
2 Heat until the apples become soft.
3 Finely chop the celery, peppers, spring onions and garlic.
4 If you are using tinned sweetcorn, drain off the water.
5 Mix all the ingredients together and leave to stand in a covered bowl overnight.

Apple Chutney

1 large apple
1 medium onion
3 tomatoes
3 sticks celery
1 green pepper
1 clove garlic
2 tablespoons raw cane sugar
2 tablespoons cider vinegar
1 level teaspoon sea salt
Freshly ground black pepper

1 Peel and grate the apple and onion.
2 Place the tomatoes in boiling water for a few seconds, remove the skins and chop.
3 Chop the celery and pepper into small pieces.
4 Slice the garlic and crush with a little salt.
5 Mix all the ingredients together in a saucepan and bring to the boil.
6 Simmer over a gentle heat for 10 minutes then remove from the heat.
7 Serve when completely cool.

Elderberry Sauce

A rich fruity sauce for cooking or use as a relish. It will keep, if properly sealed, for several years.

1 pint (570ml) berries
½ pint (285ml) wine vinegar
1 black mace
12 cloves
Ginger
1 teaspoon salt
40 peppercorns
Finely chopped onion

1 Strip the berries from the stalks with a fork and place in a large thermos flask. Pour over the wine vinegar and allow to steep overnight.
2 Next day strain off the liquor and boil in stainless steel pan with the rest of the ingredients for 15 minutes.
3 Bottle into a sterilized container and leave for one month before using.

Apple Jelly with Herbs

4 lbs (1.8kg) apples — mixed windfalls are best
Bunch fresh herbs (fresh mint, tarragon, lemon balm, lemon thyme, pineapple sage or rosemary — or a mixture of these)
½ pint (285ml) cider
Raw cane sugar as necessary

1 Quarter the apples and place in a large pan with the herbs. Add the cider and enough water so that the apples are barely covered. Bring to the boil and simmer until the apples soften.
2 Strain off the juice by passing through a jelly bag, overnight if necessary. For each pint (570ml) of juice add 1 lb (455g) of sugar.
3 Return to the pan and bring to the boil, stirring until the sugar is dissolved. Remove any scum that forms and continue boiling until a sample sets on a cold saucer.
4 Have ready a number of hot sterilized jars. Pour in the jelly and cover with a waxed disc. Seal with a cellophane jam-pot cover and label.

Variation: Mint Jelly can be made in the same way with the addition of white wine vinegar and extra mint.

Prepare the fruit as before and boil with 2 tablespoons white wine vinegar added to the water and a good bunch of applemint. After straining the juice and boiling until setting point, add 4 tablespoons finely chopped young mint leaves. Bottle immediately and seal as above.

Barbecue Sauce

This is an excellent general purpose barbecue sauce and can be used on burgers, kebabs, potatoes and vegetable dishes. It will keep for up to ten days if refrigerated.

2 oz (55g) butter
1 onion
1 clove garlic
2 tablespoons wine vinegar
¼ pint (140ml) orange juice
2 teaspoons English mustard, ready mixed
2 tablespoons soft raw cane sugar
2 slices lemon
¼ teaspoon cayenne pepper
6 tablespoons tomato purée
Few drops Tabasco *sauce*
Sea salt

1 Melt the butter in a saucepan and gently sauté the thinly sliced onion and pulped garlic for a few minutes, but do not allow to brown.
2 Add the vinegar, orange juice, mustard, sugar and lemon slices, having first removed any pips.
3 Season with cayenne pepper and bring to the boil, then leave to simmer very gently for 20 minutes.
4 Stir in the remaining ingredients and season with *Tabasco* sauce and salt to taste.
5 Allow a further 5 minutes simmering then remove the lemon slices and leave to cool. The flavour is best if left for at least 12 hours before use.

Hot Apple Sauce

This sauce is good for hamburgers and hot dogs. It can also be served cold.

1 lb (455g) cooking apples
1 small onion
2 cloves
¼ teaspoon ground ginger
Pinch cayenne pepper
4 tablespoons white wine vinegar
1 oz (30g) soft raw cane sugar
¼ teaspoon sea salt

1 Peel, core, and chop the apples.
2 Skin and slice the onion and put with the apples, spices and 2 tablespoons of vinegar into a pan.
3 Cook over a very low heat until the apples soften, then liquidize or press through a sieve.
4 Return the pulp to the pan, add the remaining vinegar and the sugar and salt and simmer gently for 10 minutes.
5 Serve whilst still hot.

Mushroom Sauce

This hot, tasty sauce is good with sausages, baked potatoes and burgers. It can be cooked beforehand and re-heated very slowly over the barbecue.

1 oz (30g) butter
1 onion
½ lb (225g) large mushrooms
1 tablespoon 81 per cent wholemeal flour
½ pint (285ml) vegetable stock
1 teaspoon yeast extract
Few drops Tabasco *sauce*
Sea salt and freshly ground black pepper

1 Melt the butter in a heavy pan and fry the finely chopped onion for a few minutes.
2 Chop the mushrooms into very small pieces and add to the pan, cooking for a few more minutes until the juice begins to run.
3 Turn off the heat and stir in the flour.
4 Cook for 1 minute, then start to add the vegetable stock, little by little, stirring constantly.
5 Add the yeast extract, *Tabasco* sauce and season to taste.
6 Simmer for 10 more minutes, then serve.

Garlic Bread

This is delicious served hot with other barbecue bread, and it's very easy to do.

1 wholemeal French loaf
4 oz (115g) butter or *polyunsaturated vegetable margarine*
2 cloves garlic
Sea salt

1 Take a sharp knife and split the loaf all the way down one side so that the two halves can be opened apart.
2 Warm the butter or margarine so that it becomes quite soft.
3 Thinly slice the garlic and sprinkle with salt then crush to a pulp with the back of a spoon.
4 Blend the garlic and butter together then spread inside the loaf.
5 Wrap tightly in a double thickness of foil and place on a moderate barbecue for 15-20 minutes, turning occasionally.
6 Unwrap, cut into slices and serve.

Garlic Rolls

Follow the instructions above, but use any wholemeal rolls of your choice instead of the French bread. Wrap each roll individually.

Herb Bread

Follow the above instructions but use only one clove of garlic and add 1 tablespoon of fresh chopped parsley and ½ tablespoon fresh chopped thyme.

Cheese and Onion Rolls

Take wholemeal rolls and split in half. Fill with a slice of cheese and a few thin slices of onion. Season with a little salt and then seal in foil and heat over the barbecue for 15 to 20 minutes.

10.

PUDDINGS

Yogurt

This healthy and versatile food is simple to make at home and does not necessarily entail buying any specialized equipment. The bacteria which convert milk to yogurt are the same as those which live inside us, helping with digestion and improving our intake of vitamins. For anyone recovering from an illness where antibiotics have been prescribed, eating yogurt is a way of re-populating with these beneficial organisms and of quickly returning the digestion to normal.

The easiest method is to use a Thermos flask, which provides ideal conditions and will produce excellent results overnight. For predictable results, a thermometer which will register temperatures around 100°F (37°C) is useful. It is important to scald the milk first, in order to kill off the normal population of bacteria which ultimately cause the milk to turn sour. A different type of bacteria is required for the yogurt-making process and this can be obtained either by buying a pure culture from a dairy or self-sufficiency suppliers or, more easily, by buying a pot of pure live yogurt. For the next few batches you can use your own yogurt, but it is best to start with a fresh culture every so often.

1 pint (570ml) milk
2 tablespoons fresh yogurt
1-2 tablespoons dried milk powder

1 Heat the milk to boiling point, then remove from the stove immediately and stand in a cool place.
2 When the milk has cooled to blood heat (98°F/37°C), stir in the natural yogurt and the skimmed milk powder.
3 Place immediately in a Thermos flask and incubate for 8 hours. Remove from the flask and refrigerate until needed. It will keep for 3-5 days.

Note: The suggested time may need some adjustment, according to the milk and the yogurt culture being used. The consistency and acidity can be controlled by varying the incubation time. Short incubation produces a mild yogurt, whilst longer incubation increases the acidity, and excessive incubation leads to separation of the whey, which should be avoided. The thickness of the finished result can be increased by adding more skimmed milk powder, or reduced by adding less, or none at all.

Fruit Yogurt

Almost any fruit, or mixture of fruit, can be used to create a variety of flavours. See the previous recipe for home-made yogurt.

1 to 2 tablespoons raw cane sugar or honey
4 oz (115g) fruit
1 pint (570ml) yogurt

1 Wash and prepare the fruit, and for larger fruits chop into small pieces.
2 Add sugar or honey to taste and cook with a lid on the pan until the juice just begins to flow.
3 Allow to cool completely and stir into the yogurt. The yogurt may be sieved or liquidized, and this is advisable for babies and children who may object to the lumps.

Hazelnut Yogurt

½ pint (285ml) plain yogurt
1 tablespoon honey
2 tablespoons hazelnuts chopped

1 Place all the ingredients in a liquidizer and blend for a short or long time, depending on how lumpy or smooth you prefer your yogurt.
2 Leave for an hour or longer in the fridge before serving, to allow the flavour to develop.

Note: A tablespoon of dried fruit added afterwards, and left to soak overnight, will also improve the flavour and make the yogurt thicker.

Fresh Fruit Salad

This dish always makes a refreshing and much appreciated end to a meal. Almost any fruit in season can be used, except soft fruits which tend to disintegrate, and in the winter some bottled or frozen fruits can be used to supplement whatever is available.

2 eating apples
2 dessert pears
Juice of 1 lemon
2 peaches
2 oz (55g) grapes
½ pineapple
1½ cups apple juice
1 tablespoon honey
2 tablespoons Kirsch (optional)
1 banana

1 Core the apples, but retain the skin, and dice into ½ inch (1.5cm) cubes.
2 Halve the pears, scoop out the cores with a teaspoon then dice in the same way. Place in a bowl and sprinkle with lemon juice immediately.
3 Halve the peaches, remove the stones and chop into small pieces.
4 If the grapes have seeds cut in half and scoop them out with a teaspoon, otherwise leave the grapes whole.
5 Peel the pineapple and remove the fibrous core, then cut into larger chunks of about 1 inch (2.5cm).
6 Mix all the fruit together in a serving bowl.
7 Mix the apple juice and honey, and add the Kirsch if used, then pour over the salad and allow to stand for at least 1 hour in the fridge. Before serving top with rounds of sliced banana.

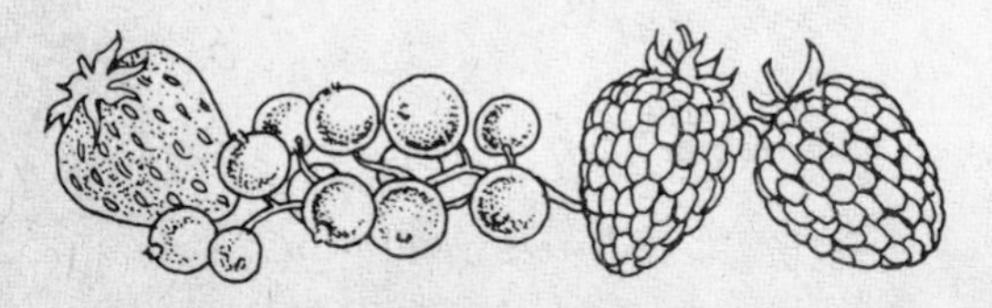

Apple Cake

2 eggs
4 oz (115g) butter
4 oz (115g) soft brown sugar
¾ lb (340g) 100% wholemeal flour
1½ teaspoons baking powder
½ teaspoon ground sea salt
½ teaspoon ground ginger
1½ cups grated cooking apple

1 Separate the egg yolks and whites and beat separately.
2 Cream the butter and sugar together and stir in the yolks.
3 Sift the dry ingredients together and add gradually to the mixture, beating well.
4 Fold the apples, together with the egg whites, into the mixture.
5 Place in an oiled shallow cake tin, lined with greaseproof paper, and bake at 375°F/190°C (Gas Mark 5) for 1 hour. Can be served hot or cold.

Fruit Crumble

Suggested fruit fillings include apple, apple and blackberry, rhubarb, cherry, plum, gooseberry, blackcurrant, etc.

For a delicious crunchy crumble replace half of the flour with crunchy muesli.

1½ lbs (680g) fruit
6 oz (170g) wholemeal flour
3 oz (85g) soft brown sugar
Pinch sea salt
3 oz (85g) butter or margarine

1 Prepare the fruit, add sugar or honey to taste and place in an ovenproof dish with a lid. Cook for 20 to 30 minutes in an oven pre-heated to 325°F/170°C (Gas Mark 3) when the fruit should be soft and the juice beginning to flow.
2 Mix the flour, sugar and salt together then rub in the fat until a crumb-like texture is achieved. Spoon this in an even layer over the fruit.
3 Increase the oven heat to 400°F/200°C (Gas Mark 6) and cook without the lid for a further 15 minutes, or until the crumble begins to brown. Serve hot or cold with cream.

Fruit Fool

This recipe works well with apples, pears, mulberries, plums and all soft fruit.

1 lb (455g) fruit
6 oz (170g) raw cane sugar (or less)
½ pint (285ml) double cream

1 Reduce the fruit to a pulp by heating gently with a little sugar, until the juice begins to flow, and then rubbing through a sieve or liquidizing. (Strawberries and banana need not be cooked.) Allow to cool completely.
2 Make sure the cream is very cold and whisk until it stands in peaks. Beware of whisking too much or your cream will turn to butter.
3 Fold the fruit pulp into the cream and divide into individual glasses or bowls and chill. Decorate with a few of the original fruits and serve with shortbread biscuits.

Fruit Pie

A good fruit pie is simple to make and always popular. It is just as appetizing hot or cold and freezes well. Suggested fillings include apple, blackberry and apple, cherry, apricot, gooseberry, blackcurrant, raspberries and rhubarb. Any shortcrust or puff pastry can be used, but the following is a good basic recipe for sweet pastry.

Sweet Pastry
6 oz (170g) wholemeal flour
½ teaspoon sea salt
½ oz (15g) raw cane sugar
4 oz (115g) butter or margarine
Ice-cold water

Filling
1½ lbs (680g) fruit
Raw cane sugar to sweeten

1 Sieve the flour, salt and sugar together into a bowl and thoroughly mix.
2 Using two knives chop the fat into the flour and rub together until small crumbs are formed.
3 Add ice-cold water, a few drops at a time, and knead until a light yet firm dough results. Cover and stand in a very cool place for a couple of hours before continuing.
4 Prepare the fruit as necessary and place in a pie dish. Use an inverted egg cup or pie crust support in the centre. Add a generous knob of butter to the filling to improve the flavour.
5 Roll out the pastry on a well-floured surface. Wet the edges of the pie dish and transfer the pastry, using a knife to press down and decorate the edges.
6 Scraps of left-over pastry can be used to decorate the crust in the form of leaves, flowers etc.
7 Brush the pastry with milk, or beaten egg, and bake in a hot oven at 425°F/220°C (Gas Mark 7) for 40 minutes, moving to a lower shelf after the first 10 minutes. Serve hot or cold with custard or cream.

Brown Rice Pudding

1 egg
1½ cups milk
2 tablespoons honey
¼ teaspoon salt
3 cups cooked brown rice
2 tablespoons raisins (optional)
Nutmeg, freshly grated

1 Beat the egg and milk together until thoroughly mixed. Add the honey and salt and beat again until dissolved.
2 Mix with the rice and raisins, if used, in an ovenproof dish and bake for 30 minutes at 350°F/180°C (Gas Mark 4). Sprinkle on the nutmeg and serve.

Honey Upside-down Cake

Topping
½ cup honey
2 oz (55g) butter
4-5 cooking apples
Maraschino cherries

Cake Mixture
1½ cups wholemeal flour
¼ teaspoon cinnamon
Pinch of ginger
½ teaspoon nutmeg
1 teaspoon baking powder
4 oz (115g) softened butter
¾ cup honey
1 egg
½ cup milk

1 Melt the honey and butter together and pour into a shallow 10-inch (25cm) ovenproof casserole.
2 Core the apples and cut into ½-inch (1cm) rings.
3 Cook the apples on both sides for a few minutes and then arrange in a neat pattern around the base of the casserole and place a cherry in the centre of each apple ring. Set aside.
4 To make the cake — sift the flour, spices and baking powder into a bowl.
5 Beat the butter and honey together in a basin and when well mixed add the egg and milk and beat again.
6 Pour this mixture into the flour and mix until smooth.
7 Cover the apples with the dough and bake in a moderate oven, 350°F/180°C (Gas Mark 4), for about 40 minutes. To serve turn out onto a plate and top with a sauce made from ½ cup honey melted with 4 oz (115g) butter. Can be eaten hot or cold.

Rice Fritters

3 eggs
½ cup cooked brown rice
2 oz (55g) currants
Grated rind of ½ lemon
¼ teaspoon nutmeg, grated
2 tablespoons raw cane sugar or honey
½ cup wholemeal flour
Vegetable oil for frying
Juice of 1 lemon

1 Beat the eggs well in a bowl and spoon in the rice, currants, lemon rind and nutmeg, with sugar or honey to taste.
2 Stir in enough flour to thicken the mixture sufficiently for frying.
3 Cook the mixture a dollop at a time in hot oil and turn to brown on both sides. If they do not brown quickly add a little more flour. Serve with a squeeze of lemon juice.

French Promises

½ pint (285ml) milk
1 egg
2 teaspoons French brandy
Pinch ground ginger
Pinch sea salt
5 tablespoons wholemeal flour
Demerara sugar

1 Beat the milk, egg and brandy in a bowl and season with a pinch each of ginger and sea salt.
2 Stir in the flour until a creamy consistency is achieved, then cook in a hot frying pan — pouring in just enough to cover the bottom and turning when golden to cook the other side. Repeat until all the mixture has been used up. Sprinkle with sugar and serve.

Friars' Omelettes

1½ lbs (680g) cooking apples
2 oz (55g) raw cane sugar
2 oz (55g) butter
2 eggs
1 teaspoon vegetable oil
½ lb (225g) wholemeal breadcrumbs
Honey to serve
Double cream (optional)

1 Peel and core the apples and cut into slices. Cook over a gentle heat, stirring in the sugar and butter. Continue cooking until soft, then remove from heat.
2 Allow to cool completely. Meanwhile thoroughly beat the eggs and when the apples are quite cold fold them in.
3 Oil an ovenproof dish or casserole and sprinkle the bottom with 1 cup of breadcrumbs. Cover with the apples and top with the rest of the breadcrumbs. Bake in a moderate oven, 350°F/180°C (Gas Mark 4), for 35 minutes and serve in slices, topped with honey and cream.

Fruit Fritters

Suitable fruits for fritters include apples, apricots, plums, bananas and pineapple.

Batter
4 oz (115g) wholemeal flour
Pinch sea salt
1 egg, separated
1 tablespoon vegetable oil
¼ pint (140ml) milk
Fruit, according to choice
Raw cane sugar

1 Sift the flour and salt into a bowl. Thoroughly mix the egg yolk into the flour with a wooden spoon.
2 Add the oil, then little by little the milk until a smooth creamy consistency is achieved. Stand for at least 2 hours in a cool place and before use fold in the stiffly beaten egg white.
3 Prepare the fruit according to variety: apples should be cored and sliced; apricots and plums can be halved and stoned; bananas can be cut into 2-inch (5cm) sections; and pineapple (if not tinned slices) should be cored and sliced.
4 Coat the fruit in sugar, to which may be added ground spices, dip in the batter and deep fry. Sprinkle with sugar and serve.

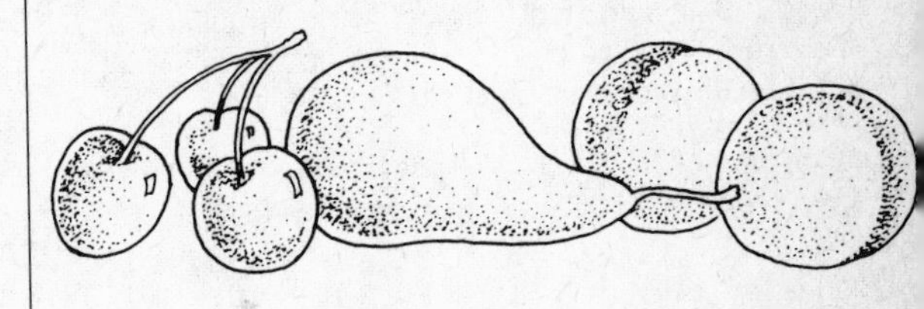

Apple Charlotte

This pudding is very good when served with an apricot sauce. The apple may also be flavoured with cinnamon or ground cloves and the receipe can be varied by adding blackberries, or any other fruit which is compatible, to the apple.

1 lb (455g) wholemeal bread
Margarine or butter, as necessary
1 lb (455g) cooking apples
Raw cane sugar to taste
1½ oz (45g) wholemeal breadcrumbs

1 Cut the bread into thin slices and remove the crusts.
2 Cut pieces of bread to line a mould or basin and then dip the bread in melted margarine or butter before putting in place in the mould. Place the coated sides against the mould, overlapping the edges and leaving no spaces.
3 Prepare the apples, cut into slices and cook with a knob of butter and sugar to taste. When the apple begins to soften at the edges remove from the heat and stir in the breadcrumbs.
4 Fill the mould with the apple mixture and cut more bread to cover the top. Bake for 30-40 minutes in a hot oven at 400°F/200°C (Gas Mark 6). Turn out onto a plate to serve.

Strawberry Shortcake

This is a delicious way of making strawberries and cream go further. The recipe also works well with fresh raspberries.

Shortcake
½ lb (225g) wholemeal flour
3 teaspoons baking powder
½ teaspoon sea salt
2 oz (55g) butter
1 tablespoon raw cane sugar, powdered in a grinder
⅓ pint (200ml) milk

Filling
1 lb (455g) strawberries
2 tablespoons raw cane sugar, powdered in a grinder
½ pint (285ml) double cream, chilled

1 Preheat oven to 450°F/230°C (Gas Mark 8) and grease two 8-inch (20.5cm) flan tins.
2 Sift flour, baking powder and salt into a bowl and rub in the butter until coarse crumbs are obtained, then mix in the sugar.
3 Make a well in the centre and pour in the milk, mixing and kneading until a smooth dough is formed.
4 Divide the dough into two, press into the tins and bake for 10 minutes until the shortcakes are golden. Allow to cool.
5 Slice half the strawberries and sprinkle over half the sugar.
6 Whip the cream until it stands in peaks. Spread half the cream over one of the shortcakes, pile on the sliced strawberries and cover with the second shortcake. Spread the remaining cream over the top shortcake and decorate with the whole strawberries and serve as soon as possible.

Chocolate Mousse

4 oz (115g) plain chocolate
4 eggs
¼ pint (140ml) double cream

1 Break up the chocolate and warm in a bowl over a pan of hot water until melted. Separate the egg whites from the yolks and beat until stiff.
2 Stir the egg yolks into the chocolate, then fold in the stiffly beaten whites.
3 Pour into individual glasses and chill to set. Top with dollops of cream.

Summer Pudding

This recipe uses whatever soft fruit is available, which can be black or red currants, raspberries, loganberries, or blackberries, or any mixture of these.

6 slices stale wholemeal bread
2 lbs (900g) soft fruit
6 oz (170g) Demerara sugar
¼ pint (140ml) double cream, to serve

1 Cut the bread, which should not be too stale, into medium-thick slices and line a 2-pint (1.1 litres) bowl or basin with it, cutting to fit where necessary so that there are no gaps.
2 Wash the fruit in a colander under cold running water. Allow to drain, then place in a pan without any additional water and stew until the juice begins to flow. Add sugar as required.
3 Pour the fruit into the basin until it is full, then cut further pieces of bread to enclose the top.
4 Find a plate which just fits inside the dish and place a small weight on it. Leave in the fridge overnight or for several hours at least.
5 When ready to eat the pudding should have set fairly solidly. To serve turn upside down onto a plate and serve with fresh cream.

Bread and Butter Pudding

This simple and homely pudding can be surprisingly delicious when made properly. A tasty variation is to add sliced banana with the raisins.

6 slices stale wholemeal bread
2 oz (55g) butter or margarine
½ lb (225g) raisins or sultanas
Grated rind of 1 lemon
2 eggs
¾ pint (425ml) milk
1 to 2 tablespoons raw cane sugar

1 Butter the bread on both sides and grease an ovenproof dish.
2 Arrange the bread in layers with the raisins and the grated lemon rind between.
3 Beat the eggs, milk and sugar until the sugar is dissolved. Pour slowly over the bread and allow to stand for 1 hour.
4 Bake in a slow oven at 300°F/150°C (Gas Mark 2) for one hour.

Honey and Raisin Steamed Pudding

A traditional and substantial steamed pudding.

4 oz (115g) butter or vegetable margarine
4 oz (115g) raw cane sugar
2 eggs
3 oz (85g) wholemeal flour
½ teaspoon baking powder
1 oz 630g) bran
4 tablespoons raisins
4 tablespoons honey

1 Cream together the fat and sugar and beat in the eggs one at a time, adding a little flour in between.
2 Fold in the remaining flour, baking powder and bran, then add the raisins.
3 Pour the honey into a well-greased pudding basin then add the pudding mixture, filling the basin to not more than two-thirds. Cover with foil and steam for 1 hour. Turn out and serve with more honey and yogurt or cream.

Honey Pancakes

Pancake Batter
4 oz (115g) wholemeal flour
½ pint (285ml) milk
1 egg
Vegetable oil for cooking
1 lemon

Honey Sauce Mix
6 oz (170g) honey
4 oz (115g) butter

1 For the pancakes: sift the flour into a bowl and make a well in the centre.
2 Add the milk and egg and incorporate the flour from the sides, then whisk. When smooth leave to stand for a few minutes.
3 Heat a little oil in a frying pan and when this is smoking pour in enough batter to cover the base of the pan. Turn when browned and when both sides are cooked, fold twice and place on a plate. Keep warm in the oven.
4 Cook the rest of the pancakes as quickly as possible and meanwhile make the honey sauce by heating the honey and butter together in a pan until blended.
5 Arrange the cooked pancakes neatly on a plate, garnishing with slices of lemon.
6 Pour over the sauce and serve onto individual plates immediately. Pancakes should be served as quickly after cooking as possible.

Pancakes with Hot Apple Purée

Make the pancakes as above, but fill with a purée made as follows:

1 lb (455g) cooking apples
Butter
Honey to taste
Chopped nuts

1 Peel, core and slice the apples and cook in a saucepan with a knob of butter and a few tablespoons of honey.
2 Stir until smooth and use to fill the pancakes. Top with chopped nuts and for a treat serve with cream.

Baked Bananas with Almonds

This surprisingly satisfying sweet is quickly prepared and bakes in the oven while you eat your first course.

4 bananas, peeled and sliced lengthways
4 oz (115g) almonds, blanched
2 oz (55g) Barbados sugar
¼ pint (140ml) double cream

1 Place the bananas in an ovenproof dish and sprinkle on the nuts and sugar.
2 Bake for 20 minutes in a moderate oven at 350°F/180°C (Gas Mark 4) and serve with dollops of cream.

Honey Tart

1 quantity sweet pastry
2 oz (55g) fresh wholemeal breadcrumbs
3 tablespoons honey
1 lemon

1 Make the pastry according to the instructions for Sweet Pastry in the Fruit Pie recipe on page 73, and use to line a plate or flan tin, retaining any left-over scraps.
2 Warm the honey very gently in a saucepan until liquid. Remove from heat and stir in the breadcrumbs, a little lemon rind and about one tablespoon lemon juice.
3 Spoon this mixture into the pastry case and spread evenly.
4 Roll out the left-over pastry and cut into thin strips. Twist and decorate the tart in a lattice pattern.
5 Cook in a pre-heated oven moderate, 350°F/180°C (Gas Mark 4) for 20-25 minutes or until cooked.

Honey Ice-cream

This recipe is very easy to make and is far superior to shop-bought ice-cream. Serve with shortbread or wafers.

1 egg, separated
4 oz (115g) honey
8 fl oz (230ml) double cream, well chilled
½ teaspoon natural vanilla essence

1 Beat the egg yolk until thick and creamy. Add the honey, little by little, and mix thoroughly.
2 Whip the cream, in a cool bowl, until it is thick and then fold into the honey and egg, together with the vanilla essence. Place in freezer until almost firm.
3 Beat the egg white and fold into the mixture, beating until smooth. Return to the freezer and stir once or twice during setting.

Variations:
1. For Hazelnut Ice Cream, add 4 oz (115g) roasted chopped hazelnuts to the above mixture after the vanilla essence has been added in stage 2.
2. For Banana Ice Cream, mash a ripe banana or two and add after the vanilla essence in stage 2. Top with a few blanched almonds.
3. Any other fruit in cooked puréed form, or finely chopped, can be added to make a fruit ice cream.

Brown Bread Ice-cream

1½ oz (45g) wholemeal breadcrumbs
1½ oz (45g) raw cane sugar
½ pint (285ml) double cream
1 oz (30g) vanilla sugar

1 Mix the breadcrumbs and the brown sugar and spread over a baking tray.
2 Bake for 15 to 20 minutes in a moderately hot oven, 375°F/190°C (Gas Mark 5), until the sugar begins to turn to caramel. Stir two or three times.
3 Allow to cool and break up into crumbs again.
4 Whip the cream and sugar together and place in the freezer.
5 When the cream is beginning to set, fold in the breadcrumb mixture and return to the freezer.
6 Leave for 15 minutes then stir again and leave to set in the freezer.

Blackcurrant Sorbet

1 lb (455g) blackcurrants
½ lb (225g) Demerara sugar
2 large egg whites
¼ pint (140ml) double cream, to serve

1 Prepare and wash the blackcurrants.
2 Add the sugar and just enough water to cover in a saucepan.
3 Bring to the boil over a gentle heat and simmer until the juice runs.
4 Sieve the fruit pulp and freeze in a shallow container for 2 to 4 hours until half frozen.
5 Remove and break up the solid portions with a fork.
6 Whisk the egg whites until stiff and fold into the syrup with a metal spoon. Return to the freezer for a further 2 to 4 hours until firm.
7 Before serving allow the sorbet to soften at room temperature for 15 minutes. Serve with whipped double cream.

Iced Fruit Mousse

Almost any fruits can be used in this recipe so long as they are prepared and cooked until they begin to soften.

4 oz (115g) fruit
1 tablespoon water
2 oz (55g) raw cane sugar
¼ pint (140ml) double cream, chilled
1 egg white

1 Heat the fruit, water and sugar in a pan, simmering gently until the fruit begins to soften. Then liquidize or sieve to produce a smooth purée and leave to cool in the fridge.
2 Beat the cream until it thickens and in a separate bowl beat the egg white until stiff. Fold the two together and then fold in the fruit purée.
3 Freeze the fruit mixture as quickly as possible. Serve scooped into glasses or bowls.

Apple Cheesecake

The richness of the cream cheese contrasts well with the sharpness of the apples in this recipe.

Pastry
3 tablespoons raw cane sugar
Pinch sea salt
½ lb (225g) wholemeal flour
5 oz (140g) butter or margarine

Filling
1 lb (455g) apples
½ lb (225g) cream cheese
1 egg
¼ pint (140ml) natural yogurt
4 oz (115g) soft raw cane sugar

1 To make the pastry case: mix the sugar, salt and flour and rub in the fat. Roll out and use to line a 12-inch (30cm) flan tin.
2 Peel and core the apples and arrange in slices in the pastry case in a neat overlapping circle.
3 Beat all the remaining ingredients together and pour over the apples.
4 Bake for 30 minutes in an oven pre-heated to 350°F/180°C (Gas Mark 4), until the top is light brown. Cool, then chill in the fridge until ready to serve.

Syllabub

This is the ideal sweet if you are looking for something special for a dinner party or festive occasion. It is also very easy to make. Add a little brandy to make it an extra-special syllabub.

1 lemon
5-6 tablespoons acacia honey
¼ pint (140ml) good white wine
1 pint (570ml) double cream, chilled
4 tablespoons brandy (optional)

1 Finely grate the lemon rind and squeeze the juice and place in a bowl with the honey and half the wine.
2 Mix well and pour in the cream, whisking until thick. Add the rest of the wine and also the brandy if you are using it.
3 Whisk again and place in individual glasses. Refrigerate before serving — this dessert can be kept for a day and is better for it.

Fruit Compote

This recipe works well with almost any fruit; quinces are particularly delicious.

4 oz (115g) raw cane sugar
½ pint (285ml) water
1 lb (455g) fruit, of any type or mixed, prepared as necessary

1 Dissolve the sugar in the water in a pan and bring to the boil.
2 Add the fruit, and once it has boiled reduce the heat and simmer gently — for 10 minutes for soft fruit, 15 minutes for apples, pears and plums.
3 Drain the fruit, reserving the juice, and place the fruit in individual glasses or bowls to serve. Meanwhile re-heat the liquid and simmer until a thick syrup is obtained. Allow this to cool, then spoon over the fruit and refrigerate. Serve with cream.

Strawberry Sorbet

4 tablespoons water
4 oz (115g) raw cane sugar
½ lb (225g) strawberries
Juice of 1 lemon

1 Heat the water in a pan and dissolve the sugar in it. Bring to the boil for a few minutes, then allow to cool.
2 Meanwhile mash or liquidize the strawberries to make a purée and add the lemon juice, then mix with the cooled syrup.
3 Place in the freezer and stir occasionally until the sorbet is set. Scoop into individual glasses or bowls to serve.

Honey-nut Custard

¾ pint (425ml) milk
4 oz (115g) honey
4 oz (115g) peanut butter
2 eggs
Pinch sea salt

1 Place all ingredients in a liquidizer and blend until smooth.
2 Pour into a greased ovenproof dish or individual cups and bake in a moderate oven, 350°F/180°C (Gas Mark 4) for 30 minutes or until set. Serve hot or cold.

11.

BREAD, CAKES AND BISCUITS

Bread

In the first part of this section are recipes, hints, and information which should enable you to make consistently good bread. The second part contains ideas and variations to try once you have mastered the basic process.

All the recipes specify 100% wholemeal flour, although they could be used with ordinary white flour with equal success. However if you are going to the trouble of making your own bread there is little point in trying to emulate the sort you can buy at any baker's. It is far better to use 100% wholemeal flour and make bread full of flavour and texture and with real character. This type of bread has been the staple diet of our land for centuries.

For many, the replacement of good hearty wholemeal bread with white, tasteless, textureless sponge has been so gradual as to go unnoticed. The big commercial concerns have progressively forced the small bakeries out of business. By using factory production methods they can make and sell bread more cheaply. But, in order to make the whole process super-efficient and super-profitable, everything has to be controllable and the flour is therefore refined and treated to remove all the variable elements. This ensures that one superloaf is identical to the next and that it remains moist and spongy down to the last slice. However, this also removes many of the nutrients and much of the vitality of the bread.

How Bread Works

The basic ingredients of bread are flour, water and salt, and unleavened bread is made just from these. However, this is too heavy for the taste of most people and a lighter, more spongy, texture is favoured. This is achieved by adding yeast, and a small amount of sugar upon which the yeast will feed, producing at the same time bubbles of carbon dioxide which blow up the dough and cause it to rise. The ability of the dough to trap this gas depends upon the gluten content of the flour. Gluten is a protein which forms elastic fibres in the dough and the more of it there is, the more the dough rises. The soluble proteins and enzymes present in wholemeal flour have an unfavourable effect upon the gluten and therefore you can never obtain quite the same 'rise' as with white dough. Wholemeal bread is therefore more solid than white and you need to accustom yourself to cutting thinner slices or eating less.

White flour is also favoured by the commercial baker because he can incorporate more water and more gas into the bread and make more loaves with less flour. Wheat flour contains most gluten and is the flour most commonly used for breadmaking.

The gluten content of different wheats varies. Canadian wheat is renowned for its hardness and is now largely imported into this country for breadmaking. British wheats are softer (less gluten) and are not favoured by commercial bakers. The idea has grown up that they are unsuitable for breadmaking. That this is not true is borne out by the fact that they have been in use for centuries and it is only in recent times that foreign wheat has been imported to any great extent. I mention this because if you are enterprising enough to grind your own grain bought from a farm, or even to grow your own, the bread will not rise as much as with shop-bought flours. It will, however, taste much better. (For information on how to grow grain see the various books on self-sufficiency by John and Sally Seymour, published by Faber.)

When buying grain to grind make sure it is not intended for planting, in which case it may have been treated with a dressing to prevent decay. If you are buying flour then the ideal sort to get is compost-grown, stoneground. This means that it is milled from grain which has been grown without the use of artificial fertilizers, insecticides, or any other chemicals. Stoneground flours are milled the traditional way with mill stones as opposed to high-speed milling with steel plates. The temperatures involved in stone grinding are lower and this helps retain more of the nutritional qualities of the grain. Such flours are available under various brand names in wholefood shops and better supermarkets. Alternatively you can sometimes find a mill or bulk wholefood supplier locally which will supply large sacks. (Look in the 'Yellow Pages' for the addresses of these.) Make sure about what exactly you are buying and ask for or buy a sample first.

Breadmaking Utensils

Breadmaking requires the minimum of utensils. The basic necessity is a large bowl, which can be bought quite cheaply from ironmongers and china shops. This should be at least 10 inches (25cm) in diameter. More pleasing, but more expensive, pottery bowls can be bought from specialist kitchen shops. Measuring jugs, spoons and scales are useful but not essential. A most useful tool is a flexible rubber or plastic spatula with which the last remnants of the dough can be scraped from the bowl. Bread tins, although not essential, are preferable as they produce a loaf which is convenient to slice. Flower pots, cake tins and a variety of other containers can be used, or just a plain baking sheet for cottage-type loaves.

Do not wash bread tins. If you oil them well with vegetable oil each time they are used they gradually develop a dark coating, which is better than any normal non-stick finish. The same goes for the baking sheet.

The Basic Bread Recipe

This method is known as the sponge method and is one which I favour because it is reliable and produces consistently good bread with most flours. It also requires minimal kneading and therefore takes less of your time. Part of its success is due to the yeast having almost ideal conditions for growth. During the initial sponge stage it is well supplied with air, which is beaten in, and it is not inhibited by the salt as in other recipes where this is added at the beginning. This method is also better for the formation of the gluten, which aids the rising process, and so is ideal for use with the softer British flours, which may prove difficult to make into good bread using any other method.

(Makes 3 medium loaves)

1½ pints (850ml) warm water
½ oz (15g) dried yeast
2 tablespoons raw cane sugar
3 lbs (1.3kg) wholemeal flour
1 tablespoon sea salt
2 tablespoons vegetable oil

1. Warm the bread bowl (at least 10 inches [25cm] in diameter) with warm water and put the measured water in the bowl. This should be at 110-115°F (43-46°C) or hand-hot. Do not use water above this temperature or the yeast will be killed.
2. Add the yeast and sugar and stir a little, but do not leave to stand.
3. Begin adding the flour straight away, stirring continuously and adding more flour until a thick creamy consistency is obtained. This is the sponge stage and you should use about half of the flour. In this method the amount of water used initially determines the total amount of flour required, as this is added until the correct consistency is achieved. As different flours vary in their capacity to absorb water it is impossible and unnecessary to give an exact quantity for the flour. Beat with a large spoon or whisk for a couple of minutes to incorporate as much air into the dough as possible, as this helps the action of the yeast.
4. Leave in a warm draught-free place to rise. In summer almost anywhere in the kitchen will be warm enough, but in winter a warmer place is desirable. The top of an Aga or other solid fuel stove is ideal. The sponge should double in size during proving. This takes 20 to 30 minutes normally and should not be prolonged.
5. Sprinkle salt over the dough and pour in the oil. Now fold in more flour, using a large spoon or spatula, and working around the edge of — rather than cutting into — the dough. Keep adding more flour until the dough becomes dry enough to handle.
6. Liberally dust your hands and the table with flour and turn out the dough. At this stage the dough may be in several small pieces mixed with dry flour, and the object is to knead all this together into one solid lump. Keep adding more flour when necessary to prevent the dough sticking to your

hands or the table. It should remain fairly moist and workable.

The technique of kneading is easily learnt. Take the lump of dough and flatten it by pressing away from you with the heels of your hands. The dough now forms a rough circle on the table. Fold this in half back towards yourself to produce a semi-circle and turn it horizontally a quarter of a turn. Push down again and fold back, repeating the same sequence of operations over and over again. Once learnt this can be done quite rapidly and with practice the separate actions merge into a continuous flowing process. Kneading is best done on a firm wooden or laminate surface. As soon as sufficient flour is incorporated into the dough stop kneading, as too much will harm the gluten.

7 Return the dough to the bowl and leave in a warm place until it has doubled in size, which should take from 20 to 40 minutes. A simple way of testing if the dough is ready is to make a slight depression with the knuckles in the dough. If the depression no longer remains after a minute or two then the dough is ready.

8 Now compress the dough with a few kneading actions and cut into three portions. Press together the cut edges of each and work in so as to leave only one seam along the bottom of each loaf. Well oil the tins or baking sheet. If using tins the dough at this stage should half fill them.

9 Leave the bread in a warm place to rise again and when risen gently transfer to the centre of a freshly lit oven set at 425°F/220°C (Gas Mark 7).

10 Cook for 45 minutes. Remove from the oven and leave to cool for a few minutes before attempting to turn out of the tins. Make certain that the bread is cooked by tapping the bottom of the loaf, which should produce a hollow sound. If the loaf is difficult to remove slide a knife around the edges. Once the tins have been used a few times there should be no trouble with sticking. It is a good idea to oil and bake new tins empty a few times. Cool the bread on top of the tins, or on a wire rack. If a thick crust is preferred on all sides the loaf can be returned to the oven for 5 minutes without the tin. Do not attempt to slice until barely warm.

Note: Do not open the oven while bread is cooking until at least 20 minutes have passed, but preferably not at all. If bread is crumbly in the centre it needs more cooking at a slightly higher temperature. This tends to happen with very large loaves. If the bread is leathery try reducing the temperature a little.

For best results do not leave any of the rising stages for too long. The minimum rising time always gives better results.

Summary of Instructions

1 Warm the bowl and put in 1½ pints (850ml) of hand-hot water.
2 Stir in ½ oz (15g) dried yeast and 2 tablespoons raw cane sugar.
3 Keep stirring and adding flour (probably about half the measured amount) until a thick creamy consistency is achieved, then beat.
4 Leave to rise for 20 to 40 minutes in a warm place.
5 Sprinkle 1 level tablespoon sea salt over the dough and pour over 2 tablespoons of vegetable oil. Fold in more flour until a hand-workable consistency is obtained.
6 With well-floured hands and table turn out dough and knead in more flour until a moist, workable, but non-sticky lump of dough is formed.
7 Return dough to bowl and leave until double in size, 20 to 40 minutes.
8 Divide the dough and form into loaves, folding under the cut edges and placing in well-oiled tins or on a baking sheet.
9 Leave to rise again for 20 to 40 minutes and gently place in the middle of a pre-heated oven at 425°F/220°C (Gas Mark 7).
10 Cook for 45 minutes, then remove and cool on a wire tray.

Decorative Toppings

To brown the bread brush the top of the loaf with milk. For a more glossy finish use an egg wash made from one egg beaten into a quarter of a cup of milk. Various seeds can be stuck onto the top of the loaf using milk or egg wash. These add extra appeal and an interesting flavour. Try the following:- poppy seeds, sesame seeds, cracked or whole wheat (soaked), sunflower seeds, caraway seeds, celery seeds or linseed.

Rolls

Follow the basic instructions (page 80) but roll out the dough into a sausage shape and divide into a number of small lumps, bearing in mind that they will double in size. Cook for only 20 minutes at the top of the oven set at 425°F/220°C (Gas Mark 7). The advantage of rolls is that they are cooked more quickly and can be served almost straight from the oven if you are in a hurry.

Plaited Loaf

When the dough is ready for the final proving divide one loaf portion into three equal-size smaller lumps and roll into three sausages about 18 inches (45.5cm) long. Press these together at one end and carefully plait, joining the other ends in the same way. Leave to rise and then brush over some egg wash and sprinkle liberally with poppy seeds. Put into the oven at the same temperature as the rest of the bread but remove after about 30 minutes.

Flowerpot Loaf

Bread can be baked in ordinary pottery flower pots and this gives it a delicious thick crust which looks most appetizing. It is best to buy a new flowerpot about 5 inches (12.5cm) in diameter. The shallow type of pot is best. Well oil and bake empty three times before using. Do not overfill or your loaf will end up in an awkward shape, unless of course you prefer a tall thin loaf!

Linseed Bread

Linseed adds a delicious oily, nutty flavour to bread. You can buy it very cheaply at a pet shop and it should be reasonably clean, although it would be safest to give it a wash in a sieve under the cold tap. Dry by spreading over a clean tea towel. Add 4-6 oz (115-170g) linseed with the second half of the flour at stage 5.

Using Other Flours

So far only wholewheat flour has been mentioned. There are, of course, a variety of other flours to choose from, although it is usually best to incorporate a certain amount of wheat flour whichever one is used. This is because all other flours have less gluten than wheat and do not rise as well. Rye and barley do have a fair amount and can be used alone to make a heavy, moist bread. Maize and buckwheat flour have none and must be mixed with some wheat flour. If you use about half and half you combine the good rising properties of the wheat and the interesting variation in texture and taste of the other. It is best to use the wheat flour to make the sponge and to add the other flour later. The following flours can all be used to make tasty bread: barley, soya, rye, rice, maize, buckwheat.

Wholegrain Bread

Wholegrains are an interesting addition and produce what is sometimes sold as granary bread. Soak wheat, barley or rye grains for at least 12 hours. Use 1 cup of dry grains to about 1 lb (455g) flour.

Enriched Breads

Eggs, milk, oils and fats can all be added to enrich bread. The water in the recipe can be all or partly replaced with scalded milk or dried milk powder can be added to the water. An egg or two can be beaten in with the water and extra vegetable oil or peanut butter can also be added. These additions tend to make the bread more smooth and moist, giving it a cake-like quality.

Other Additions

As you will begin to see, the additions which can be made to the basic dough are almost unlimited and if you use your imagination you may be able to evolve something quite new. Here is a short list of additions to give you some more ideas: chopped nuts, sunflower seeds, dried fruit, sesame seeds, rolled oats, bran, cooked rice, cooked potato (mashed), banana (mashed), grated apple or carrot, malt extract.

Note: Remember there is no need to throw away good home-made bread that has gone stale. It can be used for Summer Pudding (page 75), Bread and Butter Pudding (page 75), Croûtons (page 24) or for breadcrumbs — which are useful in a variety of dishes.

Banana Bread

Soft bananas with their skins turning black are best for this recipe and can usually be bought at cut-price at the greengrocers.

3 bananas, over-ripe
Juice of 1 lemon
4 oz (115g) raw cane sugar
4 oz (115g) polyunsaturated margarine
10 oz (285g) 100% wholemeal flour
2 oz (55g) wheatgerm
½ teaspoon sea salt
½ teaspoon baking powder
½ teaspoon bicarbonate of soda

1 Pre-heat the oven to 375°F/190°C (Gas Mark 5).
2 Mash the bananas with a fork until smooth and mix in the lemon juice.
3 Cream the sugar and margarine together then mix in the bananas.
4 Sift the dry ingredients together in a separate bowl.
5 Mix the bananas with the dry ingredients and form into a stiff dough.
6 Place in a well-greased bread tin and bake for 45 minutes or until done. Test with a knife, which should emerge clean when the loaf is done.

Scofa Bread

This is the traditional Irish soda bread and although made from wholemeal flour has a quite different texture and quality from wholemeal bread. I like it particularly for breakfast, toasted or untoasted, with marmalade or eggs.

½ lb (225g) plain 81% extraction flour
1 tablespoon baking powder
1 teaspoon bicarbonate of soda
Pinch of sea salt
1½ lbs (680g) 100% wholemeal flour
1 tablespoon Demerara sugar
1 oz (30g) butter
¾ pint (425ml) milk

1 Pre-heat the oven to 400°F/200°C (Gas Mark 6).
2 Sift the 81% flour together with the baking powder, bicarbonate of soda and salt.
3 Mix in the 100% flour and the sugar.
4 Rub in the butter until a fine breadcrumb consistency is achieved.
5 Add the milk, which should first be warmed slightly, and knead to form a stiff but smooth dough.
6 Place on a well-greased baking sheet and shape into a round loaf about 8 inches (20cm) across.
7 Using a knife, cut twice into the top of the loaf to form a cross then dust with flour.
8 Bake for one hour, when the bread should have risen and be turning golden brown on top. When cool the loaf can be broken into quarters for easy storage.

Quick Soda Bread

This is useful in emergencies when the bread runs out. It takes little time in preparation, producing quite edible results in only an hour.

½ teaspoon sea salt
2 teaspoons baking powder
½ lb (225g) 81% extraction flour
1 tablespoon raw cane sugar
½ lb (225g) 100% wholemeal flour
¾ pint (425ml) milk

1 Sift together the salt, baking powder and 81% flour.
2 Add the sugar and the wholemeal flour and mix well.
3 Add milk little by little and stir until a light dough is formed. Avoid adding so much milk that the dough becomes sticky and unmanageable.
4 Take a well-oiled bread tin and press the dough into it.
5 Bake for 45 minutes in an oven pre-heated to 400°F/200°C (Gas Mark 6). Remove from the tin and allow to cool.

Nutty Flapjacks

The quantities given for this recipe are fairly large and can of course be halved, but I find that flapjacks last no time at all unless strict rationing is imposed! Any nuts can be used.

½ lb (225g) butter or vegetable margarine
½ lb (225g) Barbados or raw cane sugar
¼ teaspoon sea salt
¾ lb (340g) rolled oats
4 oz (115g) chopped nuts
2 tablespoons sesame seeds (optional)

1 Melt the butter in a pan over a low heat and stir in the sugar and salt.
2 Mix the chopped oats and nuts in a mixing bowl and then stir in the contents of the pan and knead until of a uniform texture.
3 Press into a shallow baking tin and top with sesame seeds if liked.
4 Bake in an oven set at 350°F/180°C (Gas Mark 4) for 15 to 20 minutes or until light brown on top. Mark out the portions with a knife but do not turn out until completely cool.

Plain Honey Cake

4 oz (115g) honey
6 oz (170g) raw cane sugar
½ pint (285ml) sour milk
10 oz (285g) wholemeal flour

1 Dissolve the honey and sugar in the milk, warming a little if necessary.
2 Work the flour into this mixture, transfer to a well-greased tin and bake at 350°F/180°C (Gas Mark 4) for 45 minutes to one hour. Serve hot.

Basic Nut Cake

4 oz (115g) butter or vegetable margarine
4 oz (115g) raw cane sugar
4 eggs
4 oz (115g) wholemeal flour
4 oz (115g) chopped nuts

1 Cream the fat and sugar in a bowl and break into this one egg at a time, adding a tablespoon of flour with each egg.
2 Chop the nuts finely and add to the mixture. A few nuts can be saved for decorating the cake, either whole or coarsely chopped.
3 Now fold in the rest of the flour and place the mixture in a well-greased and lined cake tin. Bake for 1 to 1½ hours at 325°F/170°C (Gas Mark 3).

Welsh Fruit Bread

½ pint (285ml) warm water
1½ teaspoons dried yeast
1 teaspoon raw cane sugar
4 oz (115g) 81% extraction flour
¾ lb (340g) 100% wholemeal flour
3 oz (85g) polyunsaturated margarine
3 oz (85g) Demerara sugar
1 teaspoon sea salt
1 teaspoon mixed ground spice
1½ lbs (680g) mixed dried fruit
1 egg, beaten
Honey, to glaze

1 Take a bread bowl and warm it with hot water.
2 Add the warm (blood-heat) water and beat into it the yeast and sugar.
3 Add the 81% flour and beat again until a creamy mixture results.
4 Put aside for 20 minutes in a warm place, until the yeast begins to froth.
5 Place the remaining flour in a bowl and rub in the margarine.
6 Mix in the sugar, salt, spice and fruit.
7 Now add the beaten egg and the yeast mixture and mix the ingredients together with a spoon as much as possible.
8 Turn onto a floured table and knead the dough thoroughly for a few minutes.
9 Place in a covered bowl and leave to rise in a warm place until doubled in size.
10 Knock out any large bubbles with a fist then knead again. Divide into two and place in two well-greased 1 lb (455g) bread tins.
11 Pre-heat the oven to 350°F/180°C (Gas Mark 4).
12 Leave the loaves in a warm place again until the dough rises above the rims of the tins.
13 Bake for 50 to 60 minutes then glaze with honey and leave to cool on a wire rack.

Wholemeal Malt Loaf

½ teaspoon sea salt
1 lb (455g) 100% wholemeal flour
½ oz (15g) polyunsaturated margarine
2 tablespoons molasses
4 oz (115g) malt extract
½ pint (285ml) warm water
4 oz (115g) sultanas
2 teaspoons baking powder

1 Pre-heat the oven to 350°F/180°C (Gas Mark 4).
2 Mix the salt with the flour then rub in the margarine until it makes a crumbly texture.
3 In a separate bowl mix the molasses, malt extract and warm water, stirring until dissolved.
4 Mix together all ingredients except the baking powder and stir well. Leave for an hour in a warm place.
5 Sprinkle in the baking powder and stir again very thoroughly.
6 Place the dough in a greased bread tin and bake in the oven for 90 minutes.

Barm Brack

This is more of a fruit bread than a cake — not oversweet but moist, succulent and wholesome, and it is very easy to make. Save the remains of a few pots of tea; Earl Grey is particularly good, though any will do.

7 oz (200g) raw cane sugar
¾ lb (340g) mixed dried fruit
⅔ pint (340ml) cold tea
10 oz (285g) 100% wholemeal flour
2 teaspoons baking powder
1 egg

1 Soak the sugar and dried fruit in the tea overnight. Use a cloth or plate to cover.
2 Sift the flour and baking powder together thoroughly.
3 Add the tea mixture to the flour.
4 Beat the egg in a separate bowl then add and mix well until a uniform mixture results.
5 Place in a well-greased 2 lb (900g) bread tin and bake for about 1 hour 45 minutes at 350°F/180°C (Gas Mark 4).
6 Allow to cool before slicing. Serve spread with butter.

Muffins

(Makes 12 muffins)

Hungry mouths to feed for tea and not enough bread or cakes? Muffins are quick and delicious! Use special muffin rings and a baking sheet for cooking, or any small tins about 3 inches (7.5cm) across by 1 inch (2.5cm) deep. For the best muffins give the batter the minimum of mixing.

½ lb (225g) wholemeal flour
3 teaspoons baking powder
½ teaspoon sea salt
3 tablespoons raw cane sugar
4 tablespoons polyunsaturated margarine
1 egg
½ pint (285ml) milk

1 Pre-heat the oven to 375°F/190°C (Gas Mark 5).
2 Sieve the flour, baking powder and salt together in a bowl, then mix in the sugar.
3 Using two knives cut the margarine into the flour.
4 Beat the egg and milk together in a separate bowl.
5 Make a depression in the centre of the dry mixture and pour in the egg and milk.
6 Mix just sufficiently to combine wet and dry ingredients into a batter.
7 Spoon the mixture into greased muffin tins, filling to not more than half way.
8 Bake in the oven for about 20 minutes when the muffins should come cleanly away from the tin and a knife inserted into the centre should also emerge clean. Serve hot with butter.

By working from this basic recipe other tasty variations can be made, as follows:

Fruit Muffins — Add 4 oz (115g) dried fruit at stage 2.

Apple Muffins — Add 4 oz (115g) sultanas at stage 2 and beat in ½ cup of cold stewed apple with the eggs at stage 4.

Cheese Muffins — Reduce the margarine to 3 tablespoons and add ½ cup of grated Cheddar cheese in its place.

Bran Muffins — Substitute 1 cup of bran for 4 oz (115g) of the flour, 3 tablespoons of molasses for the sugar and add 2 oz (55g) of raisins at stage 2.

Spicy Muffins — To the dry ingredients add ½ teaspoon ground cinnamon, ½ teaspoon ground nutmeg, ½ teaspoon ground mace and ¼ teaspoon ground ginger.

Jam Muffins — Replace the sugar with 4 tablespoons of your favourite reduced-sugar jam or marmalade.

Banana and Walnut Muffins — Add 1 mashed over-ripe banana and 2 oz (55g) of chopped walnuts to the basic recipe at stage 5.

Hazelnut Squares

These are very easy to make as there is no cooking involved. Any chopped nuts can be substituted for the hazelnuts.

4 tablespoons set honey
4 oz (115g) chopped hazelnuts
4 oz (115g) desiccated coconut
4 oz (115g) skimmed milk powder
2 tablespoons peanut butter

1 Warm the honey in a pan and stir in the rest of the ingredients.
2 Mix thoroughly, then place in a shallow baking tray and allow to set in the fridge.

Wholemeal Digestive Biscuits

4 oz (115g) 100% wholemeal flour
4 oz (115g) medium oatmeal
Pinch of sea salt
¼ teaspoon bicarbonate of soda
3 oz (85g) butter
2 tablespoons raw cane sugar
1 small egg, beaten

1 Sieve together the flour, oatmeal, salt and bicarbonate of soda.
2 Rub in the butter until a breadcrumb consistency is achieved.
3 Add the sugar and enough beaten egg to bind the mixture and form a stiff dough.
4 Roll out on a floured board to ¼ inch (0.5cm) thickness, cut with a biscuit cutter and prick the tops.
5 Bake at 325°F/170°C (Gas Mark 3) for 15 minutes or until just beginning to brown, then cool on a wire rack.

Wholemeal Biscuits

½ lb (225g) 100% wholemeal flour
2 tablespoons 81% flour
Pinch of sea salt
¼ teaspoon mixed spice
1 oz (30g) butter
1 oz (30g) raw cane sugar
Milk

1 Pre-heat the oven to 375°F/190°C (Gas Mark 5).
2 Sieve together the flours, salt and spice and rub in the butter.
3 Mix in the sugar and enough milk to make a stiff dough.
4 Roll out thinly on a floured board and cut into biscuits with a large cutter.
5 Prick each biscuit all over with a fork and place on a well-oiled baking sheet.
6 Bake for 15 minutes or until brown, then cool on a wire rack.

Honey Biscuits

2½ oz (70g) butter
2 tablespoons raw cane sugar
2 tablespoons honey
6 oz (170g) wholemeal flour
1 teaspoon ground cinnamon
1½ teaspoons baking powder
Pinch sea salt

1 Preheat the oven to moderate, 350°F/180°C (Gas Mark 4).
2 Cream the butter, sugar and honey together and then work in the rest of the ingredients.
3 Roll out to ½ inch (1cm) thickness on a floured board and cut into 40 small rounds.
4 Bake on a well-greased tray for 10 minutes and when cool sandwich together in pairs with a little honey spread between.

Sesame Scones

Wholesome honey-flavoured scones.

½ lb (225g) wholemeal flour
½ teaspoon sea salt
2 teaspoons baking powder
2 tablespoons butter or vegetable margarine
4 tablespoons wheatgerm
2 tablespoons soft raw cane sugar
1 tablespoon sesame seeds
2 tablespoons honey
3 fl oz (90ml) sour milk or buttermilk

1 Sift the flour, salt and baking powder into a bowl and rub in the butter or margarine.
2 Mix in the wheatgerm, sugar and half the sesame seeds, and then the honey and milk.
3 Knead until a dough is formed. Shape into a round about ¾ inch (2cm) thick and cut into 4 portions.
4 Sprinkle with the rest of the sesame seeds and bake on an oiled baking sheet for 10-15 minutes in a hot oven, 425°F/220°C (Gas Mark 7). When cooked, split in half, butter and serve whilst still warm.

Sesame Squares

This recipe is ideal for young children to make as no cooking is involved.

4 tablespoons honey
4 oz (115g) sesame seeds
4 oz (115g) desiccated coconut
4 oz (115g) skimmed milk powder
2 tablespoons peanut butter

1 Melt the honey and stir in the other ingredients until well mixed.
2 Place in shallow greased trays or flan tins and refrigerate until set.

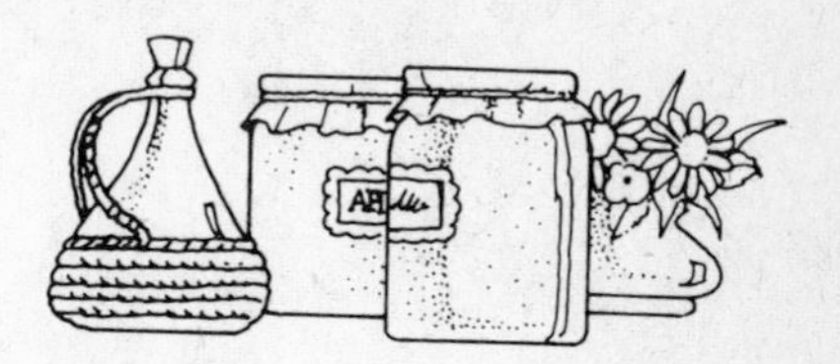

Index

Index

Index

Of further interest . . .

THE VEGETARIAN COOKBOOK

Everything from Starters to Sweets

400 of the greatest variety of vegetarian meals you are ever likely to find anywhere. Includes everything from Brazil Nut and Tomato Roast to Digestive Biscuits. **Doreen Keighley**, in conjunction with the Vegetarian Society of the United Kingdom, has here produced a superb collection of recipes tried and tested throughout many years of vegetarian cooking. She includes invaluable information on freezing the completed dishes and microwave defrosting as well as vital nutritional advice. Seasonal recipes such as Christmas Cake, Simnel Cake and Hot Cross Buns are treated to new invigorating recipes which are wholefood, vegetarian, high-fibre and low in fat and sugar and all are presented in a clear and easy-to-read style. *A great present — if you can bear to give it away!*

HAPPINESS IS JUNK-FREE FOOD

An excellent and long overdue volume which supplies practical nutritional advice for the, understandably, anxious parents of problem children. There is now very real evidence to *prove* that food additives are causing actual damage to some children. In the absence of clear medical directives to the parents of such children this 'junk-free' recipe book has been produced by **Janet Ash and Dulcie Roberts**. You may not think YOUR child is affected, but you won't *know* unless you experiment by cutting out 'junk' foods. This book shows how to do it without causing your child to riot at the sudden absence of the food he/she has come to know and love.